AF488040

Decoding National Education Policy 2020

Implemenation, Adaptability & Challenges

Editor

DATTA G SAWANT

Xpress Publishing
An Imprint of Notion Press

Xpress Publishing

An Imprint of Notion Press

India. Singapore. Malaysia.

First Published by Notion Press, April 2024

ISBN 9798894151946

Made with ❤ on the Notion Press Platform

www.notionpress.com

Dedicated to all the honest teachers

who work to transform the society

Contents

Preface

Wisdom was lost without education
Without wisdom morals were lost
Without morals progress was lost
Without progress wealth was lost
Without wealth Shudras were ruined
Such havoc was imposed by ignorance.

-Mahatma Jyotiba Phule

Education is one of the highly powerful tools through which we can transform a society and ultimately, a nation. Education cultivates the mind and intellect of human being living in a society. It enforces the capabilities of understanding good and bad, profound and mean in a society. No nation could progress without the proper system and implementation of education. It is crucially significant to have a robust and all inclusive system of education for any nation who wants to build the pillers of development in different sectors. The development of a nation is highly based on the education system they carry. Looking at India with this perspective, it is one of the third largest education systems in the world which required a revamp to cope with the current situation. India has had policies on education before and after independence that paved the way in framing Indian education system. After the reforms of 1986 Policy on Education, the National Education Policy 2020 is the major stepping stone in the sector of education. The National Education Policy 2020 or simply NEP 2020 has the ability to transform the whole system and strengthen the youth of the nation. The bill of NEP 2020 has been passed in the Parliament on 29th July 2020 and its implementation began in the academic year 2023-2024. Maharashtra is one of the leading states in the country to implement the NEP 2020 in higher education.

The present volume of chapters is an outcome of the ICSSR WRC, Mumbai sponsored one-day national conference on National Education Policy 2020: Adaptability & Challenges organised by the Department of English, Toshniwal Arts, Commerce & Science College, Sengaon, Dist. Hingoli, Maharashtra on 17th Febraury, 2024. The research articles sent for presentation in the conference modified into full length chapters and suitably edited to fit for the publication.

As it is said in the title of the book, the chapters try to provide an insight into the provisions, implementation, outcomes and overall, the effect of the policy on whole education system, in a way decoding the policy at length. The chapters' like Academic Bank of Credits: Adaptability and Challenges, Role of Teachers in NEP 2020, NEP 2020: A Critical Analysis of its Impact on Higher Education in Maharastra, Legal Education Through Window of NEP 2020: An Analysis, Exploring the Integration of Home Science Curriculum within the NEP Framework, Crucial Role of India's National Education Policy 2020 in Shaping the Present Era, so and so forth directly shed light on various aspects of the policy.

I hope the book will provide useful knowledge about the policy to the readers including students, teachers, researchers, policy implementers, and stakeholders of higher education.

Datta G Sawant
10.05.2024
Sengaon

Acknowledgments

The present book is an outcome of the national conference based on the theme National Education Policy 2020: Adaptability & Challenges organised by Department of English, Toshniwal Arts, Commerce & Science College, Sengaon funded by ICSSR, WRC, Mumbai. The warm regards go to the Director, ICSSR, WRC, Mumbai for allocating the fund for the one-day conference.

It is my pleasure to thank the Chairman of SGSPM Mr. Brijgopalji Toshniwal, the CDC Chairman Mr. Ramanji Toshniwal, the Principal Dr. S.G. Talnikar, the Head of the Department Dr. Rajesh Gore and all the staff members of Toshniwal Arts, Commerce & Science College, Sengaon for their support in organising the conference and editing the book.

I would like to extend the warm regards towards all the contributors of this volume for sending their chapters and papers with due corrections.

I specially thanks to Notion Press Media Pvt. Ltd. for accepting the proposal for publication and publishing the book Decoding National Education Policy 2020: Implimentation, Adaptability & Challenges.

Editor

1. Academic Bank Credit: Adaptability and Challenges

Dr. Rajesh S. Gore

Introduction

Academic Bank Credits is closely associated with the University Grants Commission (UGC) and National Education Policy (NEP) 2020. UGC is a governing body in Higher Education that has played an important role in developing and implementing Academic Bank Credits in India. The NEP 2020 is a comprehensive policy framework mainly aimed at transforming the education system in India. It has contained the concept of Academic Bank Credits as means of promoting flexibility and credit mobility in higher education. It promotes new national education policy 2020s vision creating a flexible and student-centric education that enables them to pursue their academic interests and career aspirations as per their own choice. It allows students to accumulate and transfer his/her credits from one institution to other institutions for educational purpose. The Academic Bank of Credits system enables them to access a wider range of educational opportunities that helps them to save their time and money in the process of taking education.

Academic Bank Credits (ABC) is a virtual (digilocker) platform where students can see his/her academic credits on virtural platform. It is a kind of formal system through which a student can recognize his/her credits and credit can transfer from one institution to another and redemption of his/her earned credits in their academic or the educational life. It is accountable for students in opening, closing and validation their academic bank credits using digilocker app from playstore. It offers freedom to the learners in choosing their courses in education. Students can access his/her credits anywhere without manual help because it is available in virtual mode. Both online and offline courses are included in the academic bank credits. The credits accumulated by the students in ABC will be valid for only seven years for his/her educational or academic purpose. The Academic Bank of Credits is promoting flexibility and credit mobility in higher education. This book chapter is trying to discuss the various dimensions and challenges in adapting the Academic Bank Credits.

Education plays a very crucial role in shaping the minds of young ones and turning them into learned citizens. Education paves the way for the young and learned people to live life confidently and effectively. We have seen how the education system of India has been working since ancient times. Education was given in formal and informal ways; education was given at home, temple, pathshala and gurukula. The National Policy on Education was formed by the Government of India to promote and regulate education in India. The first National Policy on Education was declared by the Government of India under the leadership of Indira Gandhi in 1968. The second National Policy on Education came into existence under the leadership of Rajeev Gandhi in 1986. The NPE 1986 was modified in 1992 by P. V. Narasimha Rao. The third National Education Policy (NEP-2020) was promulgated under leadership of Narendra Modi in 2020. The central government of India put the proposal of National Education Policy 2020 (NEP 2020) in the cabinet of Central Government. It approved in the meeting of Central Cabinet of Government of India on 29th July 2020 by taking responses or feedbacks from different kinds of stakeholders from the society. The draft of National Education Policy is based on MHRD's draft of 2019. The policy relies on the five basic components such as access, quality, accountability, equity and affordability. The National Educational Policy is a general framework which focuses on the transformation of the entire Indian education system. The main objective of NEP 2020 is to transform the education system up to 2040 and increase studnet enrollment ratio by 50% up to 2050. The new education policy is a unique in its nature for its implementation. In NEP-2020, the old structure of education 10+2+3+2 is replaced by a new structure 5+3+3+4. In the draft of NEP 2020, we prominently come across the restructuring or reframing of higher education. It promotes a multidisciplinary approach in bachelor degree with multiple exit and multiple entry options. It avails freedom for students to select multidisciplinary subjects or courses from the given basket of subjects. The student has to select courses such as Major, Minor, Discipline Specific Courses, Generic Electives, Ability Enhancement Courses, Indian Knowledge System and Co-Curricular Courses. The new policy brought the new concept of Academic Bank Credits to promote flexibility and credit mobility to the learners in higher education. It creates a new vision of creating a more flexible and student centered education system that is able to pursue their academic interests and career opportunities in future. It helps UGC's effort to streamline credit transfer smoothly and creates a seamless education system across the country. It also helps to create uniformity in the entire Indian education system. The book chapter focuses on various dimensions and challenges in adapting the Academic Bank Credits.

Academic Bank Credits is based on the National Academic Depository (NAD). It is the backbone of Academic Bank Credits where the academic information like marks, grades, rewards and transfer certificates of students are stored. The students can access any academic information with the help of Digilocker. NAD provides a platform for ABC that facilitates students to create ABC ID which can be used to store, transfer, redeem and receive recognition for academic credits. Now, the University Grants Commission (UGC) has made it compulsory for all the universities and colleges to create ABC ID of their students. UGC appeals to all the learners in the education system to take benefits of this innovative system. By creating ABC ID, students can access their account information, check their academic progress and manage their credits online. This allows greater freedom to the students and avails them various academic opportunities with flexibility. The learners can transfer his academic credits to another institution, pursue a different degree, select courses for individual enrichment through Academic Bank Credits. It is a major step in achieving students' academic and career goals. The institutes affiliated to the Universities can easily avail the facility of ABC ID to their students. Academic Bank Credits provides more flexibility to the students to choose their learning path and gives freedom to move from one institution to another without losing their earned credits. The students who are unable to complete their education at one place, so he can complete his education at the place where he moved due to his/her personal reason.

Scope & Nature of Academic Bank Credits (ABC)

Academic Bank Credits is close to the University Grants Commission (UGC) and National Education Policy 2020 (NEP 2020). Academic Bank Credits (ABC) is introduced to the students to make their teaching-learning smooth in Higher Education. It is a virtual (digilocker) platform where students can see his academic credits. It is a kind of formal system through which a student can recognize his/her credits, credit can transfer from one institution to another and redemption of his/her earned credits in their educational life. It is accountable for students in opening, closing and validation their academic bank credits using digilocker app from playstore. It offers freedom to the learners in choosing their courses in education. Students can access his/her credits anywhere without manual help because it is available in virtual mode. Both online and offline courses are included in the academic bank credits. The credits accumulated by the students in ABC will be valid for only seven years for his/her educational or academic purpose. The Academic Bank of Credits is promoting flexibility and credit mobility in higher education. By offering the free hand to the learners to accumulate and transfer his/her credits from one institution to another institution. It enables them to access a wide range of education opportunities and helps them to save time and money.

National Credit Framework (NRF) is an educational qualification framework in higher education, vocational skill and school education. However, the creditization and integration is in higher education supporting the certificate/diploma/ degree with the concept of multiple entry and exit options must follow the National Credit Framework.

Academic Bank Credits (ABC) is a system by which the coursework like theory/practical/tutorial/training is measured. The required number of instructional hours per week is determined by it.

Semester of (13-15 Weeks)	Theory/ Week	Tutorial/ Week	Practical/Week	Training/ Week
1 Credit	1 Hr.	1 Hr.	2 Hrs.	1 Week of internship

It functions as a credit bank, by allowing students to borrow academic credits from one institution to another to complete their degree requirements. It allows students to transfer credits from one institution to another by providing a transparent and efficient process for transferring academic credits. Students can obtain credits earned from various institutions and programs to allow them to build a comprehensive academic profile. The Academic Bank Credits system validates credits earned by the students in his/her academic career. ABC serves as a central repository of all academic credits earned by the students and makes it easy to access and share their academic records with other institutions.

Functions of ABC

Academic bank credit is a system that promotes academic mobility and flexibility to the students by providing an opportunity to create their own individual learning paths and enabling institutions to fetch the attention of a wider range of students. It has a certain kinds of functions like:

1. ABC is accountable for opening, closing and validation of academic credits of students.
2. It works as credit accumulation, credit verification, and credit transfer/redemption of studetns.
3. The online and offline courses offered by government and other recognized institutes like SWAYAM, NPTEL and MKCL etc.
4. The validity of these earned credits will be up to seven years. Students can redeem these credits for his academic purpose. The student has to join his/her academic journey within those seven years.
5. ABC credits can be redeemed at any stage. Students can take direct admission to the second year at any university in India.

The academic bank credits will be work as shown in the following figure:

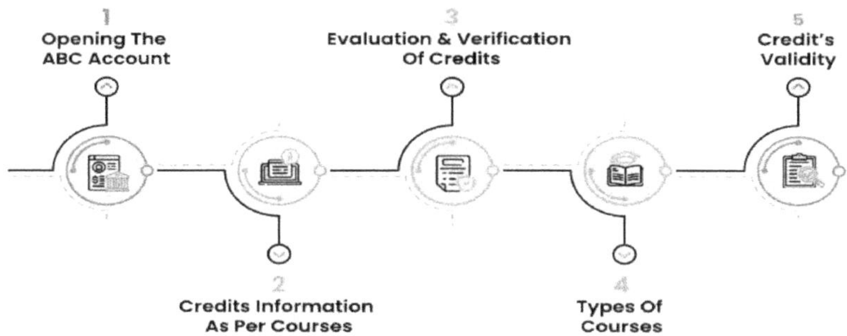

The above are the process of ABC functioning. The student has to open his/her ABC account first to enter into an academic venture. Academic Bank Credits works as:

Academic Bank Credits provides the flexibility and mobility to create a unique path for every individual. It works as credit management for students and institutions through Academic Bank Credits. "Credits awarded to a student for one program from an institution may be transferred/ redeemed by another institution upon students' consent". Credit transfer is the key to successful study mobility.

Academic Bank Credits is a general system of credit recognition, credit accumulation, credit transfer and credit redemption. It helps students to accumulate his/her credit from earlier learning experiences. It is providing students mobility across Higher Education Institutions. The credits earned by the students in his/her academic year will be deposited to their academic bank credits. However, the students are facing certain challenges to open their ABC account through Digilocker. The students should well aware with digilocker so that he can create his/her own account to create ABC ID. If you are a student, you have to be a part of Academic Bank Credits by creating your ABC ID as follows:

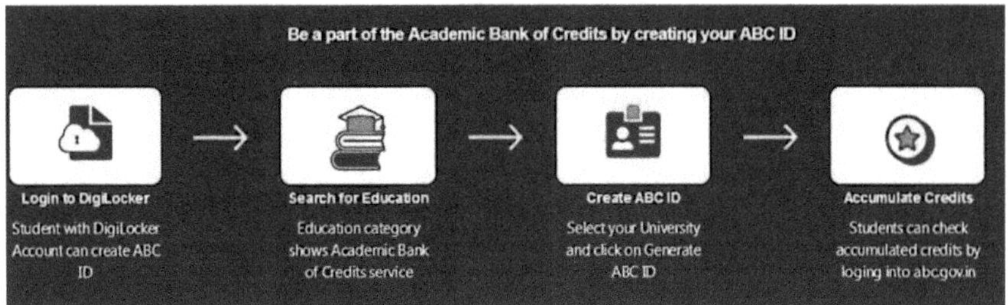

While starting the academic journey as a student with this new National Education Policy 2020. At the time of admission, students have to register for their ABC ID. Students can create his/her account to login Digilocker to create their ABC ID. Firstly, a student has to join the Academic Bank of Credits tab on Digilocker to create an ABC ID and accumulate his/her academic credits in this bank. After clicking the join button, the new interface will appear before you as Academic Bank of Credits. In that interface, students he will have to fill some information like Name (as per aadhar), Date of Birth (16/08/2002), Gender (male/female), Identity Type (New Admission), Identity Value (05081980), Admission Year (2024), Institution Name (University Name) and then get your ABC ID. Students can check their credits by login to abc.gov.in or Digilocker.

Challenges of Academic Bank Credits

At the very outset, when the students, teachers and educators heard about the ABC ID, they were a little bit confused about this upcoming term Academic Bank Credits in NEP 2020. There are certain kinds of challenges faced by students while opening his/her ABC ID. These challenges are as follows:

Awareness with ABC ID: Students are not well aware of the term Academic Bank Credits. They have to understand how the Academic Bank Credits works, how the credits are earned, accumulated and redeemed. They don't even know the validity of credits. They have a number of questions in their minds regarding ABC ID- What is credits? What is the management system of Academic Bank Credits? How does a student open their account to generate their ABC ID? The students are not well aware with the ABC ID.

Issues of Technology: Technology is one of the leading problems before the students to create their ABC ID. The students living in the rural areas are facing serious concerns because they don't have android phones. If they had they would be facing network issues. They could not generate their ABC ID's through android phones. Some of the students do not know how to install apps on their phones and how it works.

Authentication of Aadhar: The student can create his/her ABC ID to login Digilocker on their android phones. For the login to Digilocker, the student has to link his/her mobile numbers to aadhar to create their account on the Digilocker. If the authentication of aadhar is not done properly they will not be able to create their account. The students don't have the knowledge to link their mobile phones to aadhar. While facing this problem of aadhar authentication, the student has to go again to the E-Seva center to link their mobile numbers with aadhar. It will take time of fifteen days to link their mobile numbers with aadhar. However, it is one of the hurdles in the way to create an ABC ID. Authentication of Aadhar is mandatory to create ABC ID of students.

Pressure to create an ABC ID: At initial level of the academic year, the unnecessary pressure given to the students to create their ABC IDs. It is mandatory for everyone to know the credits earned because it is crucial for their academic progression. It creates high pressure on the students to accumulate his/her credits in the learning process. The students are not well aware about the new system of Academic Bank Credits. Hence, the unncecssary burden of this new system is increased on the minds of students. Teachers, Principals, Institutions, Managements and Governments can relieve pressure of students by making their orientation about the new system of Academic Bank Credits.

Equality and Accessibility: Equality and accessibility are the key pillars of National Education Policy 2020. It is one of the big challenges to ensure students who have an equal opportunity to earn credits in Academic Bank Credits system. If the criteria to earn credits is not all inclusive and students are facing some problems to access the available resources.

Concern for Documentation and Record Keeping: The students have a serious concern about their documentation and record keeping that will be available on the Academic Bank Credits. Students don't know how to track their accumulated credits and their academic achievements are properly documented within the ABC system.

Conclusion

The ABC system provides credit mobility between partnering institutions. For credit mobility between institutions, the National e-Governance Division (NeGD) of the Ministry of Electronics and Information Technology (MeitY) has developed the ABC platform under the Digilocker framework. The ABC shall provide the facility and functionality for a student to open an academic account and to get a valid platform to register in Higher Education. The ABC is a digital platform to store the academic credits. The students can earn his/her credits from higher education institutes registered with the bank and provide appropriate data for HEIs to award degrees, diplomas, PG diplomas and certificates as merited by the students over a particular period of time. The ABC will also ensure the opening, closing and validation of credits, credit verification, credit accumulation and credit transfer and redemption for students. All Higher Education Institutes are mandatory to register in the ABC to enable credit mobility of students. It is a need of time to make an orientation of the new system of Academic Bank Credits to students by teachers, institutions, government organizations and other education agencies.

References:

Academic Bank Credits: Ministry of Education, Government of India. https://www.abc.gov.in/ Accessed on 10th April, 2024.

Bhandari Mukund Shriram. International Journal of Innovative Research in Technology, *"New Education Policy (NEP) and Academic Bank Credit (ABC)"*, Vol.10, Issue 12, May 2022.

https://ijcrt.org/papers/IJCRT2209265. Accessed on 3rd Feb., 2024.

https://ijirt.org/master/publishedpaper/IJIRT155066_PAPER. Accessed on 5th Feb., 2024.

https://www.iitms.co.in/blog/what-is-academic-bank-of-credit. Accessed on 6th April, 2024.

https://www.researchgate.net/publication/373195831_Benefits_of_the_A cademic_Bank_of_Credits_ABC_According_to_New_Education_Pol icy_NEP_2020. Accessed on 6th February, 2024.

Killedar, Sangram. *"Benefits of the Academic Bank of Credits (ABC) According to New Education Policy (NEP 2020)"*, edited in Revamping Libraries in Modern Era, PRARUP PUBLICATION, 2023.

Nathani, Poonam. *What is Academic Bank Credits (ABC) in Higher Education Institutions.*

Pathak Vinay Chandra. International Journal of Creative Research Thought, *"Academic Bank of Credit an Initiative for the Flexibility in India's Higher Education System"* Vol.10, Issue 9, September 2022. Pp. 71-73.

The Academic Bank of Credits: A New Pathway to Higher Education https://www.eklavvya.com/blog/academic-bank-credits/#Introduction Accessed on 20th March, 2024

The Academic Bank of Credits: A New Pathway to Higher Education. https://www.eklavvya.com/blog/academic-bank-credits/ Accessed on 10th April, 2024.

2. Role of Teacher in NEP 2020

Dr. Pranjali Bhanudas Vidyasagar

Introduction

Nantional Education Policy 2020 (NEP 2020) mandates that the learning should be holistic, integrated, inclusive, enjoyable, and engaging. In order to minimize rote learning and to encourage holistic development and 21st century skills such as critical thinking, creativity, scientific temper, multilingualism, problem solving, ethics, social responsibility and digital literacy; curriculum, textbooks, pedagogy and assessment at all stages of school education shall be transformed. It stresses that in all stages, experiential learning will be adopted, including hands-on learning, arts-integrated and sports integrated education, story-telling-based pedagogy, among others, as standard pedagogy within each subject, and with explorations of relations among different subjects. To close the gap in achievement of learning outcomes, classroom transactions will shift, towards competency-based learning and education. (Para 4, NEP 2020).

In this process it is essential to understand the innovative ways of teaching and showcase, disseminate and replicate the innovative strategies of successful teachers. The teaching community must coordinate, work well together, and be driven by a desire to change students' lives via the development of their skills and character, as the NEP is implemented on the ground. The new education policy must help re-establish teachers, at all levels, as the most respected and essential members of our society, because they truly shape our next generation of citizens.

Changing Role of Teacher in NEP-2020

The recently released National Education Policy (NEP) is to be implemented in phases beginning 2021. In the past decades, we have seen similar policy recommendations such as the Kothari Commission, many that are yet to be implemented. A critical review of two earlier policies indicates there are gaps in implementation and limited training for educators. NEP recommends restructuring of the entire education domain of India. It talks about foundational literacy and numeracy and skill education to transform India to face 21st century challenges. The success of any education policy rests upon the belief and efforts of its' fraternity.

Educators must be proactive in understanding in detail the ethos, the aims, objectives and the motto of the NEP and upskill themselves with rigorous Continuous Professional Development programs, trainings, participation in seminars, workshops and conferences at various levels. Implementation of NEP will require discarding the age-old practices of memorization and rote learning and adopting Constructivist pedagogies to go beyond textbooks and the aim must be to change from syllabus completion to achieving learning outcomes. Educators must understand and embrace the concepts of integrated and multidisciplinary approaches and the need for development of 21st century skills. The NEP emphasizes the teacher's contribution, their sacrifice and efforts to uphold the dignity, respect and honor of this profession.

Teachers will be given more autonomy in choosing aspects of pedagogy, so that they may teach in the manner they find most effective for the students in their classrooms. Teachers will also focus on socio-emotional learning - a critical aspect of any student 's holistic development. The NEP 2020 acknowledges the reality of unmotivated and dispirited Indian teacher and proposes to completely overhaul the teaching profession to create robust merit based structure of tenure, salary, and promotion, that incentivizes and recognizes outstanding teachers. The National Educational Policy recognizes and identifies teachers and faculty as the heart of the learning process. The Policy will empower teachers of India and lists out various reforms for their recruitment, continuous professional development, service conditions etc. NEP recommends restructuring of the entire education domain of India. It talks about foundational literacy and numeracy and skill education to transform India to face 21st century challenges. The success of any education policy rests upon the belief and efforts of its' fraternity.

Educators must understand and embrace the concepts of integrated and multidisciplinary approaches and the need for development of 21st century skills. Multidisciplinary and holistic learning is an innovative medium through which the teachers can learn sciences, technologies, mathematics with liberal arts, humanities, languages, social sciences, professional skills, vocational skills, ethics, morality, human values and so on at the same time. It aims at overall development which means now teachers can have knowledge or mastery across fields through access to information and communication technology, teacher trainings and other facilities at the higher education institutes and newly introduced MERUs (Multidisciplinary Education and Research Universities).

Multidisciplinary Approach: A New challenge to Teachers

The Multidisciplinary approach also known as a shared model, connects two or more disciplines such as math and science (Fogarty, 1991). Multidisciplinary instruction is an approach that thoughtfully incorporates and connects key concepts and skills from many disciplines into the presentation of a single unit. The multi-disciplinary approach moves up the curriculum ladder by thinking these disciplines under one problem or theme, but without making any conscious connections between the subjects. The connections come within the discipline content and are only connected to other disciplines by the common theme. For-example teaching a science unit on simple machines and a social studies unit on the industrial revolution under the common theme of change is an example of using a multidisciplinary approach (Fogarty,1991).

Challenges to Teachers in View of NEP 2020

The Policy appears impressive in its outlook but the actual challenge lies in its very implementation. Multiplicity of boards and total inequality in their content and standard are other major obstacles. But biggest challenge is going to be formulation of revised curriculum and pedagogy at each of the four (04) stages of education and its actual delivery at ground level. Considering the fact India has one of the biggest diverse school educations in the world with more than 1.5 million schools and around 250 million students with dissimilar background, this is going to be a nightmare.

Changing the mindset of around 10 million school teachers many of whom are from rural background is going to be another major obstacle. Lack of accreditation at school level currently is the other issue of quality check that needs to be tackled. Intention of the government may be serious and good with lofty idea to take India to the next orbit but making it happen is going to the real challenges. The National Education Policy 2020 aims at building a global best education system rooted in Indian ethos, thereby transforming India into a global knowledge superpower.

In collaboration with parents and other key local stakeholders, teachers will be more involved in the governance of schools/ school complexes, including as members of the School Management Committees/School Complex Management Committees.

To help ensure that schools have positive learning environments, the role expectations of principals and teachers will explicitly include developing a caring and inclusive culture at their schools, for more effective learning for all, and for the benefit of all in their communities.

Teachers will be given more autonomy in choosing finer aspects of pedagogy, so that they may teach in the manner that they find most effective for the students in their classrooms and communities. Teachers will focus on socio-emotional learning, which is a critical factor in any student's holistic development. Teachers will be recognized for novel approaches to teaching that improve learning outcomes in their classrooms.

Teachers will be given constant opportunities for self-improvement and to learn the latest innovations and advances in their profession. To ensure that every teacher has the flexibility to optimize their own development as teachers, a modular approach to continuous teacher development will be adopted. Developmental opportunities, in the form of local, state, national, and international teaching, and subject workshops, as well as online teacher development modules, will be available to all teachers so that each teacher may choose what is most useful for their own development.

Through the NEP, there will be an evident transition wherein the transitional classrooms and the teaching-learning process will now emphasis on conceptual development and not a transaction, experiential learning in real-world contexts and an enabler for developing essential ethos and values in the digital age. The teachers are envisioned to educate and empower the country. To prevent the large amounts of time spent currently by teachers on non-teaching activities, teachers will not be engaged any longer in work that is not directly related to teaching in particular, teachers will not be involved in electioneering, cooking of midday meals, and other strenuous administrative tasks, so that they may fully concentrate on their teaching-learning duties.

Conclusion

The importance of developing 21st-century abilities as well as integrated and interdisciplinary methods must be understood by educators. The teaching community must coordinate, work well together, and be driven by a desire to change students' lives via the development of their skills and character, as the NEP is implemented on the ground.

The National Education Policy (NEP) that came into effect in 2020 proposes a complete restructuring of the Indian educational system with a particular focus on fundamental reading, numeracy, and 21st-century skills to prepare students for what lies ahead. However, while it suggests the changes and modifications, it also highlights that the success of much of the Policy depends on the competence of the teachers who will be taking the reforms forward.

National Education Policy 2019 will play an important role in the transformation of the Indian education system. Now it is expected to help India in reaping its demographic dividend. NEP will play a significance role for development of pre-primary education to higher education system in India. The present paper had studied the National policies and the interrelation to the teachers. Also, the present paper focused on role of teacher, as a Teacher is to shape the minds of the younger generation. The students- teacher interaction is very significant in the new education era. Also study some observations related to NEP 2019.

References

Aggarwal, J.C. (1986). *National Policy on Education 1986 and Main Recommendations of National Commissions on Teachers*. Doabs House.

Digumarti, B.R. (2000). *Education for All: Achieving the Goal: Issues and Trends.*

MHRD. (1974). Ministry of Human Resource Development. Integrated Education for Disabled Children (IEDC) Programme. Department of Higher Education.

MHRD. (1997). Ministry of Human Resource Development. District Primary Education Programme (DPEP). Progress Overview.

MHRD. (1998). Ministry of Human Resource Development. National Policy on Education 1986: as modified in 1998 with National Policy on Education 1968. Government of India, Department of Education.

MHRD. (2004). Ministry of Human Resource Development. Sarva Shiksha Abhiyan: A Programme for Universal Elementary Education: Manual for Planning and Appraisal. GOI, Department of Elementary Education and Literacy.

MHRD. (2005). Ministry of Human Resource Development. Inclusive Education: Action Plan for Inclusive Education of Children and Youth with Disabilities. GOI, Department of Higher Education.

NEP 2020. https://www.mhrd.gov.in/sites/upload_files/mhrd/files/nep/

Prasad, J (2007). *Principles and Practices of Teacher Education.* Kanishka Publishers.

Sharma, S.P. (2016) *Teacher Education. Principles, Theories and Practices.* Kanishka Publishers.

Shore, J.R. (2004). *Teacher Education and Multiple Intelligences: A Case Study of Multiple Intelligences and Teacher Efficacy in Two Teacher Preparation Courses.*

Singh, R. P. (1983). *The Nature of Teaching.* National Publishing House.

Thakur, D.N. (1995). *Impact of Education Policy in India.* Kanishka Publishers.

Yadav, B. (2010). *Education and Development.* Anil Kumar Thakur and Mohan Patel (Eds.). *Challenges of Education in 21 Centuries.*

3. NEP 2020: A Critical Analysis of its Impact on Higher Education in Maharashtra

Rajendrakumar Ahirrao and Narender Paul

Introduction

India's education system is undergoing a major transformation with the adoption of the National Education Policy 2020 (NEP 2020). The NEP 2020 is a comprehensive and holistic policy that covers all levels and domains of education, from pre-primary to higher education. The policy aims to create a learner-centric, flexible, and inclusive education system that fosters creativity, innovation, and excellence. The policy also seeks to align the education system with the national goals of social justice, economic development, and global integration. The NEP 2020 has been widely praised by various stakeholders, including the central and state governments, educational institutions, academicians, experts, and students, for its vision and ambition. However, the policy also faces some challenges and criticisms, especially in terms of its implementation, feasibility, and impact. In this review, I will critically examine the impact of NEP 2020 on higher education in Maharashtra, one of the most populous and developed states in India. Maharashtra has a rich and diverse educational sector, with some of the leading universities and colleges in the country. The state has also been a pioneer and leader in educational reforms, contributing significantly to India's educational progress. The state has shown a keen interest and enthusiasm in implementing the NEP 2020 in its higher education sector. The state government has formed various committees and sub-committees to develop a roadmap and guidelines for the implementation of the policy. The state has also identified 144 autonomous educational institutions that will start implementing the NEP 2020 from the current academic year 3. The state has also revised its curriculum and credit structure for undergraduate and postgraduate programs in accordance with the NEP 2020. The NEP 2020 offers several opportunities and benefits for higher education in Maharashtra. The policy can help improve the quality, access, and equity of higher education in the state, by introducing more flexibility, choice, and diversity in the curriculum and pedagogy. The policy can also help foster a culture of innovation, research, and entrepreneurship among the students and faculty, by creating a conducive environment and infrastructure for multidisciplinary and interdisciplinary learning. The policy can also help enhance the employability and skill development of the graduates, by aligning the education system with the needs and demands of the society and the economy. However, the NEP 2020 also poses some challenges and risks for higher education in Maharashtra. The policy requires a huge amount of financial, human, and technical resources for its effective implementation, which may not be readily available or sufficient for the state. The policy also requires a significant amount of coordination, collaboration, and consensus among various stakeholders, such as the central and state governments, the regulatory bodies, the educational institutions, the teachers, the students, and the parents, which may not be easy or smooth to achieve. The policy also entails a radical shift in the existing norms, practices, and traditions of the education system, which may face some resistance or opposition from some sections of the society, especially those who are accustomed to or benefit from the status quo. Therefore, the NEP 2020 is a visionary and ambitious policy that has the potential to transform the higher education sector in Maharashtra, but it also requires careful planning, execution, and evaluation to ensure its success and sustainability. The state government and the educational institutions should work together to address the challenges and leverage the opportunities that the policy offers, while also ensuring that the policy is responsive and adaptive to the local context, needs, and aspirations of the people of Maharashtra. The NEP 2020 is not a one-size-fits-all solution, but a framework that can be customized and contextualized to suit the diverse and dynamic realities of the state. This review aims to provide a comprehensive and balanced perspective on the NEP 2020 and its impact on higher education in Maharashtra.

Review

The implementation of significant policy changes in higher education institutions is a complex process that involves various stakeholders, challenges, and adaptations. India's National Education Policy (NEP) of 2020 represents a comprehensive reform aimed at transforming the country's educational landscape. This literature review explores the existing body of knowledge regarding the challenges faced and adaptability demonstrated by higher education institutions in Maharashtra during the implementation of the NEP 2020.

Policy Implementation in Higher Education: Historically, the implementation of educational policies has been a multifaceted challenge. Smith and Lipsky (1993) argue that policy implementation is a dynamic process influenced by the interactions between policymakers, implementers, and the organizational context. The success of any policy reform depends on how effectively institutions navigate these interactions [1].

Challenges in Policy Implementation: Policy implementation in higher education faces various challenges. Prakash and Umesh (2018) highlight administrative hurdles, faculty resistance, and resource constraints as common impediments. The adaptability of institutions to policy changes is contingent upon their ability to address these challenges [2].

Faculty Adaptation and Resistance: Faculty members play a pivotal role in the successful implementation of educational policies. A study by Cohen, March, and Olsen (1972) emphasizes the importance of faculty buy-in and highlights potential resistance due to perceived disruptions in established routines. Understanding the factors influencing faculty adaptability is crucial for effective policy execution [3].

Organizational Culture and Change: The organizational culture of higher education institutions significantly influences their capacity to adapt to policy changes. Bolman and Deal (2017) argue that successful change efforts align with the existing culture and values of an organization. Assessing the impact of the NEP 2020 on the organizational culture of Maharashtra's universities is essential for understanding adaptability [4].

Student Perspectives and Experiences: Students are key stakeholders in higher education, and their experiences shape the success of policy implementation. Trowler (2010) discusses the importance of considering student expectations, feedback mechanisms, and involvement in decision-making processes to enhance adaptability and satisfaction [5].

Comparative Analysis of Clustering Initiatives: The clustering of universities is a strategy increasingly employed to foster collaboration and resource-sharing. Insights from international experiences, such as the University of California's Merced Cluster (Dougherty, Natow, & Vega, 2017), offer valuable lessons for understanding the potential benefits and challenges associated with clustering in the context of Maharashtra's NEP implementation [6].

Issues of NEP 2020

- Early streaming of scholars into totally different disciplines.
- Lack of access to HE, particularly in socioeconomically underprivileged areas that resulted within the current gross enrollment magnitude relation (GER) of twenty fifth solely.
- Lack of teacher and institutional autonomy to create innovations in HE to draw in several students.
- Insufficient mechanisms for career management and progression of school and institutional leaders.
- The lack of analysis and innovations at the most of schools} and colleges. Suboptimal levels of governance and leadership at pedagogy establishments. A corrupted regulative system permitting faux schools to thrive whereas constrictive glorious, innovative establishments.

Analysis of Data

District Wise Distribution of Universities, Colleges and Standalone Institutes:

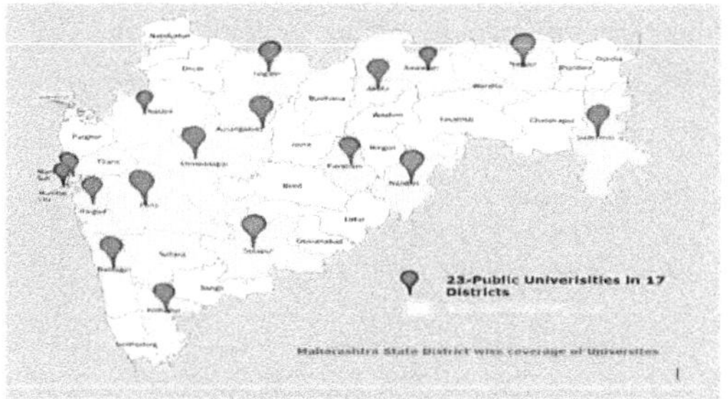

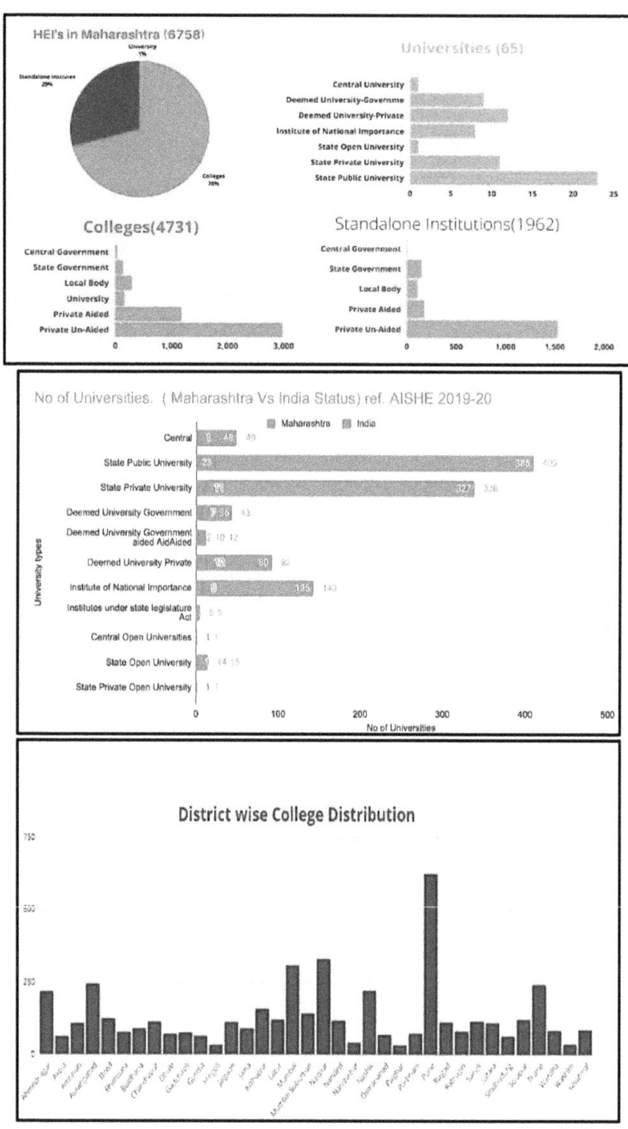

The graphs show some statistics about the higher education sector in Maharashtra and India, based on the AISHE 2019-20 report. Here are some possible interpretations:

The first graph suggests that Maharashtra has a lower share of universities in the country, especially in the categories of central, state public, and deemed universities. This could indicate a lack of diversity and autonomy in the higher education system of Maharashtra, as well as a possible gap in funding and quality.

The second graph indicates that there is a high concentration of colleges in one district, which could be Mumbai, the capital and largest city of Maharashtra. This could imply an uneven distribution of educational opportunities and resources across the state, as well as a potential challenge for rural and remote students to access higher education.

Maharashtra higher education ranking

Maharashtra is one of the leading states in India in terms of higher education, with a large number of universities and colleges offering various courses and programs. According to the EduRank website, Maharashtra has 53 universities ranked among the best in India, with the highest-ranked one being the Indian Institute of Technology Bombay at number 1. Maharashtra also has several prestigious research institutes, such as the Tata Institute of Fundamental Research and the Institute of Chemical Technology. However, Maharashtra also faces some challenges, such as the low share of universities in the country, the uneven distribution of colleges across districts, and the quality and relevance of education. According to the NIRF website, Maharashtra has only 8 universities in the top 50 in India, and only one central university. The state also has a high concentration of colleges in Mumbai, which could limit the access and opportunities for students from other regions. Moreover, the state needs to improve the quality and innovation of education, as well as align it with the goals of the National Education Policy 2020 [11].

Educational status of Maharashtra as compared to other states in India

Maharashtra has one of the highest literacy rates in India, with 82.3% as per the 2011 census[12].Maharashtra has also performed well in the Performance Grading Index (PGI) 2019-20, a tool to assess the quality of school education in India. Maharashtra, along with Kerala and Punjab, achieved the highest score of 928 out of 1000, placing them at level 2 out of 10 [13].However, Maharashtra has also faced some challenges in the recent years, such as the decline in reading ability among surveyed children from 44.2% in 2018 to 26.1% in 2022, as per the Annual Status of Education Report (ASER) 2022 [14]. The COVID-19 pandemic and the subsequent lockdowns have also disrupted the education system and affected the learning outcomes of students [15-16].

Karnataka government denied to implement NEP 2020

According to the web search results, the Karnataka government has decided to scrap the National Education Policy 2020 (NEP) from the next academic year and replace it with a new State Education Policy (SEP). The chief minister Siddaramaiah has cited the following reasons for this decision [17-18]:

- NEP is incompatible with the federal system of governance and undermines the Constitution and democracy.
- NEP has several anomalies and flaws that encroach upon the state's rights and prerogatives in the domain of education.
- NEP does not suit a diverse nation like India, which has different religions, languages and cultures.
- NEP has been opposed by various stakeholders, including students, parents, teachers and lecturers.

The Karnataka government intends to craft a new education policy that aligns with its vision and values, and addresses the needs and aspirations of the state's students and educators. The new policy will also consider the human rights, constitutional values, and the Right to Education. The state government has also expressed the need for a clear long-term vision and a nuanced approach in policy formulation1[19-20].

Criticism of NEP 2020

The NEP 2020 is a new policy that aims to reform the Indian education system, but it also faces some challenges and criticisms from various stakeholders. Some of the common criticisms are:

- The policy may not be feasible or affordable for the state governments and the educational institutions, as it requires a huge amount of financial, human, and technical resources for its implementation [21-22].

- The policy may not be inclusive or equitable for the students from different linguistic, cultural, and socio-economic backgrounds, as it promotes the use of mother tongue/local language as the medium of instruction until grade 8 [23-24].
- The policy may not be compatible or consistent with the existing laws and regulations, such as the Right to Education Act, 2009, which mandates free and compulsory education for children between 6 and 14 years of age [25].
- The policy may not be responsive or adaptive to the local context, needs, and aspirations of the people of different states and regions, as it imposes a uniform and centralized framework for the education system [26-27].

These are some of the major criticisms of NEP 2020, but there may be other perspectives and opinions as well.

Challenges in Implementing NEP 2020 in Maharashtra

The National Education Policy 2020 (NEP 2020) holds the promise of transforming India's education system, striving for inclusivity, flexibility, and quality. However, the implementation of this ambitious policy in Maharashtra, like in many other states, encounters a series of challenges that demand careful consideration and strategic solutions [28-32].

Funding Woes: NEP 2020 calls for a significant increase in education spending, aiming to raise the allocation from 4.6% to 6% of the GDP. For Maharashtra, this translates to an additional requirement of INR 1.5 lakh crores over the next five years. The economic impact of the ongoing Covid-19 pandemic exacerbates the challenge, necessitating a delicate balance between the policy's financial requirements and the state's fiscal constraints.

Linguistic Quandaries: While NEP 2020 encourages the use of local languages as the medium of instruction until grade 5, the decision is left to the states. In Maharashtra, the official language is Marathi, but a shortage of Marathi textbooks for the new academic session highlights the practical challenges in implementing the language policy. Ambiguities in language preferences among stakeholders add another layer of complexity.

Curriculum Overhaul: NEP 2020 proposes a comprehensive overhaul of the curriculum, including the integration of Indian knowledge systems, multidisciplinary courses, and a credit-based system. This necessitates a massive effort in curriculum development, teacher training, and updating of learning materials. In Maharashtra, committees and sub-committees have been formed to address these challenges and redesign the curriculum across various subjects and levels.

Infrastructure Deficits: Ensuring universal access to quality education requires a significant upgrade in physical and digital infrastructure. However, many schools and colleges in Maharashtra, particularly in rural areas, lack basic facilities like internet connectivity and computers. Addressing these deficits is crucial for meeting the standards set by NEP 2020.

Equity and Inclusion Imperatives: NEP 2020 emphasizes equity and inclusion, demanding special attention to the needs of marginalized groups. In Maharashtra, students face challenges such as poverty, discrimination, and violence, leading to higher dropout rates among certain communities. Bridging these gaps requires targeted interventions, including scholarships, fee waivers, and a supportive educational environment.

Coordination Conundrum: Effective implementation of NEP 2020 requires seamless coordination among diverse stakeholders. However, Maharashtra has faced challenges in coordinating with the central government and other states, particularly concerning language policies, regulatory frameworks, and funding mechanisms. Establishing robust mechanisms for consultation and conflict resolution is essential.

As Maharashtra grapples with these challenges, it is crucial for the state government and educational institutions to view them not only as obstacles but also as opportunities for innovation and improvement. Collaborative efforts, flexibility in approach, and a keen understanding of local nuances will be pivotal in successfully implementing NEP 2020 in Maharashtra. The policy is not a rigid blueprint but a framework that can be tailored to meet the unique dynamics and aspirations of the state, ensuring a transformative impact on the education landscape.

Navigating Challenges

Lack of Clarity in Funding Distribution:
Criticism: Maharashtra's approach to sharing increased education expenditure between central and state governments remains unclear.
Statistic: The current state of education funding in Maharashtra, which may not align with the proposed 6% of GDP target.
Delay in Implementation Plan:
Criticism: Maharashtra lacks a clear plan for the implementation of NEP 2020, leading to potential delays and hindrances.
Statistic: Despite the policy being in place, a concrete roadmap for execution is yet to be established.
Persisting Educational Funding Issues:
Criticism: Maharashtra has struggled to achieve the 6% of GDP goal since the Kothari Commission's report in 1960, and current funding cuts may further impede progress.
Statistic: Maharashtra's historical funding trends and recent reductions in educational funding.
Exclusionary Practices Impacting Minorities:
Criticism: There's a need for Maharashtra to address the exclusionary aspects of NEP 2020, especially concerning minorities.
Statistic: Lack of specific provisions and efforts in Maharashtra to ensure equal opportunities for minority groups.
Unaddressed Inequity in Medium of Instruction:
Criticism: Maharashtra's implementation of NEP 2020 does not sufficiently address the issue of inequity arising from the medium of instruction.
Statistic: Ongoing challenges related to language-based inequalities in Maharashtra's education system.
Potential Privatization Concerns in Higher Education:
Criticism: Maharashtra's implementation of NEP 2020 might inadvertently lead to the privatization of higher education.
Statistic: Trends in autonomy and affiliation changes in Maharashtra's colleges and universities.
Risk of Intellectual Colonization:
Criticism: Maharashtra needs to be cautious about potential intellectual colonization, where the policy might primarily benefit the affluent.
Statistic: Socioeconomic trends and educational patterns in Maharashtra that may contribute to intellectual colonization.

Impact on Caste and Class-Based Inequalities:

Criticism: Despite the policy's ideal intentions, there's a risk that Maharashtra's implementation might exacerbate caste and class-based inequalities.

Statistic: Existing educational disparities and demographic data related to caste and class in Maharashtra.

Operational Complexity in School Infrastructure:

Criticism: Maharashtra's plan for school complexes may face operational challenges in regions with low student numbers.

Statistic: Operational complexities and resource distribution concerns in Maharashtra's diverse regions.

Teacher Deployment and Shortage Challenges:

Criticism: Maharashtra's response to the steep rise in teacher shortages should include comprehensive recruitment and retention strategies.

Statistic: Maharashtra's teacher shortage data and proposed deployment measures.

Ambiguity in Maharashtra's School Regulation Approach:

Criticism: The creation of an independent State School Regulatory Authority may lack historical precedent and pose challenges in Maharashtra.

Statistic: Lack of established models or successful precedents for regulatory separation in the state.

Resolving Challenges in Implementing NEP 2020 in Maharashtra

Funding:

Advocacy and Collaboration: Create a collaborative platform involving education policymakers, state officials, and financial experts to advocate for increased funding for education at the national level. Establish dialogues with the central government to negotiate a fair distribution of funds based on the specific needs and performance indicators of Maharashtra.

Public-Private Partnerships: Explore opportunities for public-private partnerships to supplement government funding. Encourage private enterprises to invest in education through CSR initiatives and partnerships with educational institutions.

Capacity:

Faculty Development Programs: Implement comprehensive faculty development programs to enhance the skills of existing educators and attract new talent. Encourage the participation of educators in workshops, seminars, and training programs to familiarize them with the multidisciplinary approach envisaged in NEP 2020.

Infrastructure Upgrade: Develop a strategic plan for upgrading educational infrastructure across the state. Allocate resources to create new institutions and enhance existing ones, focusing on creating a conducive environment for diverse disciplines.

Governance:

Stakeholder Consultation: Facilitate discussions and consultations with stakeholders, including state governments, to define the roles and autonomy of state-level bodies in conjunction with HECI and its verticals. Ensure that the new governance structure aligns with the local context and addresses the unique needs of Maharashtra's education system.

Transitional Period: Implement a gradual transition to the new governance structure to minimize disruptions. Develop clear guidelines for cooperation between state and central bodies during the transition phase.

Culture:

Curriculum Localization: Invest in the development and refinement of curriculum content in local languages, emphasizing the inclusion of regional perspectives. Collaborate with experts in linguistics and cultural studies to ensure the quality and relevance of content.

Inclusive Pedagogy: Train educators in inclusive pedagogical practices that integrate local culture into teaching methods. Encourage the use of diverse teaching materials and assessment tools that reflect the cultural richness of Maharashtra.

Monitoring and Evaluation:

Regular Audits: Establish a robust monitoring and evaluation system to assess the progress of NEP 2020 implementation in Maharashtra. Conduct regular audits of institutions to ensure adherence to quality standards and accreditation requirements.

Feedback Mechanism: Implement a feedback mechanism involving students, faculty, and industry representatives to gather insights into the effectiveness of NEP 2020 initiatives. Use this feedback to make continuous improvements and adjustments to the implementation strategy.

By addressing these challenges through a combination of policy advocacy, strategic planning, and stakeholder engagement, Maharashtra can navigate the complexities of implementing NEP 2020 and harness the opportunities for educational enhancement in the state.

Findings

The review of the literature and data on the impact of NEP 2020 on higher education in Maharashtra reveals that the policy offers several opportunities and benefits, as well as challenges and risks, for the higher education sector in the state. The opportunities and benefits include:

- Improving the quality, access, and equity of higher education in the state, by introducing more flexibility, choice, and diversity in the curriculum and pedagogy.
- Fostering a culture of innovation, research, and entrepreneurship among the students and faculty, by creating a conducive environment and infrastructure for multidisciplinary and interdisciplinary learning.
- Enhancing the employability and skill development of the graduates, by aligning the education system with the needs and demands of the society and the economy.

The challenges and risks include:

Funding: The policy requires a huge amount of financial, human, and technical resources for its effective implementation, which may not be readily available or sufficient for the state. The state government has estimated that it will need an additional INR 1.5 lakh crores over the next five years to implement the policy.

Language: The policy encourages the use of local languages as the medium of instruction at least upto grade 5, but also leaves it to the states to decide the language policy3. This creates ambiguity and confusion among the stakeholders, such as the parents, the teachers, and the students, who may have different preferences and expectations regarding the language of learning. Moreover, the availability and quality of teaching-learning materials and assessment tools in local languages is also a concern. For instance, the state has faced a shortage of textbooks in Marathi, the official language of the state, for the new academic session.

Curriculum: The policy proposes a major overhaul of the curriculum, which includes the integration of Indian knowledge systems, the introduction of multidisciplinary and flexible courses, the adoption of a credit-based system, and the alignment with the learning outcomes framework3. This requires a massive effort to develop, revise, and update the syllabi, the textbooks, the pedagogy, and the evaluation methods, as well as to train the teachers and the administrators to cope with the changes. The state has formed various committees and sub-committees to review and redesign the curriculum for different subjects and levels.

Infrastructure: The policy aims to provide universal access to quality education, which implies the need to expand and upgrade the physical and digital infrastructure of the educational institutions. This includes the construction and maintenance of classrooms, laboratories, libraries, hostels, toilets, playgrounds, etc., as well as the provision of electricity, water, internet, computers, tablets, etc. However, many schools and colleges in Maharashtra, especially in rural and remote areas, lack the basic facilities and resources to meet the standards and expectations of NEP 2020. For example, according to a survey, only 28% of the schools in the state have internet connectivity, and only 12% have computers.

Equity: The policy strives to ensure equity and inclusion in education, which means addressing the diverse needs and aspirations of the learners, especially those from the disadvantaged and marginalized groups, such as the girls, the SCs, the STs, the OBCs, the minorities, the differently-abled, etc. This involves the provision of scholarships, fee waivers, reservations, remedial classes, counseling, etc., as well as the promotion of a culture of respect, tolerance, and diversity in the educational institutions. However, many students in Maharashtra face various barriers and challenges in accessing and completing their education, such as poverty, discrimination, violence, migration, etc. For example, the dropout rate among the tribal students in the state is 16.7%, which is higher than the national average of 13.5%.

Coordination: The policy requires a high degree of coordination and collaboration among various stakeholders and agencies involved in the education sector, such as the central and state governments, the regulatory bodies, the academic councils, the universities, the colleges, the schools, the teachers, the parents, the students, the industry, the civil society, etc. This necessitates the establishment and strengthening of effective mechanisms and platforms for consultation, communication, and cooperation, as well as the resolution of conflicts and disputes, if any. However, the state has faced some issues and challenges in coordinating with the central government and other states on various aspects of the policy, such as the language policy, the regulatory framework, the funding mechanism, etc.

These are the main findings of the review, which indicate that the NEP 2020 is a visionary and ambitious policy that has the potential to transform the higher education sector in Maharashtra, but it also requires careful planning, execution, and evaluation to ensure its success and sustainability. The review also suggests that the state government and the educational institutions should work together to address the challenges and leverage the opportunities that the policy offers, while also ensuring that the policy is responsive and adaptive to the local context, needs, and aspirations of the people of Maharashtra. The review also identifies some gaps and limitations in the existing literature and data on the topic, which can be addressed by future research.

In conclusion, the adoption of NEP 2020 in Maharashtra holds immense promise for reshaping the state's higher education landscape. The critical analysis underscores the enthusiasm within the state for embracing the policy's objectives of learner-centric, inclusive education. However, the identified challenges, spanning financial constraints, coordination issues, and societal resistance, necessitate strategic solutions. The recognition of NEP 2020 as an opportunity to enhance education quality, accessibility, and employability is crucial. The study emphasizes the need for collaborative efforts, meticulous planning, and customization to align the policy with Maharashtra's diverse educational context. By addressing funding uncertainties, linguistic complexities, curriculum revisions, infrastructure deficits, equity concerns, and coordination challenges, Maharashtra can navigate the obstacles and successfully implement NEP 2020. The proposed solutions presented in the conclusion serve as a roadmap for policymakers, urging them to approach challenges as catalysts for innovation and positive transformation in the state's education sector.

References

A reality checks on NEP 2020: 6 major challenges in implementation. (2020). India Today, New Delhi.

Ashok Kumar, P. (June 2023). *Implementation of NEP 2020 in Higher Education: Challenges & Way Forward.* TheRise.co.in

Bhawna, M. (August 2023). *Challenges for Rural Institutions in Adopting NEP 2020 And Their Solutions.* International Journal of Information Movement, 8(IV), 28-31.

Bhikhubhai, P. J. (October 2022). *A CRITICAL STUDY OF NEP 2020.* IJCRT | Volume 10, Issue 10.

Bolman, L. G., & Deal, T. E. (2017). *Reframing organizations: Artistry, choice, and leadership.* John Wiley & Sons.

Chandwani, S. (2020). *National Education Policy 2020: Challenges and Criticism.* BW Businessworld

Cohen, M. D., March, J. G., & Olsen, J. P. (1972). *A garbage can model of organizational choice.* Administrative Science Quarterly, 17(1), 1-25.

Darbar, T. P. (2021). *Impact of National Education Policy 2020 on Higher Education.* IJCRT | Volume 9, Issue 5.

Dhokare, C. S., Jadhav, S., & Gaikwad, A. (December 2022). *Transforming Higher Education: Exploring the Impact of NEP 2020 Implementation in India.* International Journal of Food and Nutritional Sciences; Volume 11, Issue 12.

Dougherty, K. J., Natow, R. S., & Vega, B. L. (2017). *Creating a new university in the United States: Entrepreneurship as a cultural system.* Higher Education, 73(1), 89-106.

Education in Maharashtra - Wikipedia.

Education Statistics and Growth Figures Year-wise of Maharashtra– Indiastat.

Educational Statistics At A Glance; Government Of India Ministry Of Human Resource Development Department Of School Education & Literacy Statistics Division New Delhi 2018.ESAG-2018.pdf (education.gov.in)

ESAG-2018.pdf (education.gov.in)

Five Charts on the Status of School Education in India (thewire.in)

Governor, *Minister review preparedness of Universities for implementing NEP from coming Academic Year* (Jan. 2023). Raj Bhavan Maharashtra | India. Link

Hazarika, T. (July 2020). *NEP 2020 Key Takeaways for Higher Education: 4 Yr UG Education.* Single Regulator. MPhil. Discontinued. Jagran Josh.

Higher and Technical Education Department Government of Maharashtra; Higher and Technical Education Department Government of Maharashtra, Ministry of Higher and Technical Education.

Karnataka Government to Replace NEP 2020 With New State Education Policy (Aug 22, 2023).

Karnataka to implement its own education policy in place of NEP. (Jul 08, 2023).

Karnataka to scrap NEP 2020 implementation for next academic year. TOI Education (Aug 17, 2023).

Maharashtra: *NEP 2020 rollout challenges* - EducationWorld

NEP Task Force report.pdf (maharashtra.gov.in)

NEP to be scrapped in state from next academic year says Karnataka CM (Aug 15, 2023).

Prakash, A., & Umesh, U. N. (2018). *Policy implementation in higher education in India: A case of self-financing engineering colleges.* Higher Education for the Future, 5(1), 48-68.

Prakash, N. (May 20, 2023). *Maharashtra: NEP 2020 rollout challenges.* EducationWorld

Rai, S. (August 2020). *National Education Policy (NEP) | A critical look at NEP-2020.* Telegraph India

Singh, R. (n.d.). *New Education Policy: Advantages & Disadvantages.* IndiaTimes

Smith, S. R., & Lipsky, M. (1993). *Nonprofits for hire: The welfare state in the age of contracting.* Harvard University Press.

Top Universities in Maharashtra | 2023 University Ranking | uniRank (4icu.org)

Trowler, P. (2010). *Student engagement literature review.* The Higher Education Academy, 1-16.

Wasil, F. A. (November 2022). *A critical insight into NEP 2020.*

4. Exploring the Implications of NEP 2020 for Individuals with Learning Disabilities

Arjun Namdevrao Khobragade

Introduction

The NEP 2020 has been a topic of much discussion and debate in India since its announcement. While the policy aims to create a more robust and inclusive education system in India, little attention has been paid to the implications of this policy on individuals with learning disabilities. Learning disabilities affect at least 10% of the populations in India, and it is vital to analyze how the new policy will affect their education. Therefore, this paper aims to explore the potential impact of NEP 2020 on individuals with learning disabilities and analyze the areas that may need modification to ensure their academic success. The paper starts by providing an overview of NEP 2020, followed by a brief introduction to learning disabilities. The paper then discusses the implications of NEP 2020 for individuals with Learning Disabilities and provides recommendations for policymakers to address their needs. Overall, this paper highlights the essentiality of inclusive education through NEP 2020 that benefits every child, regardless of their abilities.

NEP 2020: An Overview

The National Education Policy (NEP) 2020 is a comprehensive policy that aims to bring the transformational changes in the Indian education system. The policy aims to provide accessible, inclusive and equitable education to all students. It is designed to meet the needs of the 21st century and to address the challenges faced by the Indian education system.

NEP 2020 envisages a new structure of education that would emphasize on early childhood education and care, foundational literacy and numeracy, a flexible multi-disciplinary undergraduate education model, and a holistic approach to learning to equip every student with the skills, knowledge, and values needed to lead a productive life.

The policy aims to promote critical thinking, creativity, communication, collaboration, and digital literacy among students. It also stresses the importance of vocational education, skill development, and entrepreneurship education to equip students with the necessary skills to find self-employment opportunities.

NEP 2020 aims to integrate technology in education and pedagogy, along with bridging the gap between urban and rural education. It recognizes the role of indigenous knowledge and language in education, and the need for the development of local languages.

Overall, NEP 2020 envisions India's education system to be an inclusive and holistic system that enables students to pursue their interests and passions while preparing them for the future.

Some of the key highlights of NEP 2020

• A 5+3+3+4 structure of school education, with the first five years of primary education being the foundation stage, the next three years being the preparatory stage, and four years of secondary stage.

• Introduction of a new curriculum and pedagogical framework, which emphasizes on holistic, multidisciplinary and experiential learning.

• Provision of early childhood care and education, to ensure universal access to quality education form age 3 onwards.

• Expansion of vocational education and skill training to develop employability skills in students from an early age.

• Emphasis of mother tongue/local language as the medium of instruction till grade 5, and gradually moving towards multilingualism.

• Establishment of a new National Education Technology Forum to ensure the integration of technology in teaching – learning

• Increased emphasis on teacher training and professional development.

• Establishment of a National Research Foundation to promote research and innovation in education.

• Promotion of internationalization of education, by collaborating with global institutions and attracting foreign students for higher education in India.

The implementation of NEP 2020 is expected to bring about transformation changes in the Indian education system, which will lead to an improved academic performance, enhanced employability and a more inclusive and equitable society.

Learning Disability: A Brief Overview

Learning disabilities refer to a range of neurological disorders that affect an individual's ability to learn and process information. Learning disabilities are not linked to intelligence, but rather to the brain's functioning in specific areas such as reading, writing, and math. Common reading disabilities include dyslexia, dyscalculia, dysgraphia, language processing disorder, and non-verbal learning disorder. Students with learning disabilities may have difficulty with memory, attention, organization, and problem solving skills. Learning disabilities are not related to intelligence or motivation, and individuals with these disabilities can have average or above-average intelligence. Early identification and intervention can help individuals with learning disabilities overcome challenges and achieve success in school and life.

Some Common Types of Learning Disabilities

Dyslexia: Dyslexia is a learning disability that affects a person's ability to read, write, and spell. Individuals with dyslexia may have difficulty with word recognition, decoding, and comprehension.

Dysgraphia: Dysgraphia is a learning disability that affects a person's ability to write. Individuals with dysgraphia may have difficulty with handwriting, spelling, and organizing their thoughts on paper.

Dyscalculia: Dyscalculia is a learning disability that affects a person's ability to understand and manipulate numbers. Individuals with dyscalculia may have difficulty with basic arithmetic, understanding mathematical concepts, and applying math in real-life situations.

Auditory Processing Disorder: Auditory Processing Disorder (APD) is a learning disability that affects a person's ability to understand and process sounds. Individuals with APD may have difficulty understanding speech in noisy environments, following directions, and distinguishing between similar sounds.

Visual Processing Disorder: Visual Processing Disorder (VPD) is a learning disability that affects a person's ability to interpret visual information. Individuals with VPD may have difficulty with visual-spatial tasks, such as reading maps, understanding graphs, and recognizing shapes.

Nonverbal Learning Disabilities: Nonverbal Learning Disabilities (NLD) is a learning disability that affects a person's ability to understand nonverbal cues and social interactions. Individuals with NLD may have difficulty with nonverbal communication, spatial awareness, and recognizing social cues.

Attention Deficit Hyperactivity Disorder: Attention Deficit Hyperactivity Disorder (ADHD) is a learning disability that affects a person's ability to focus and control impulses. Individuals with ADHD may have difficulty with organization, time management, and completing tasks.

Autism Spectrum Disorder: Autism Spectrum Disorder (ASD) is a learning disability that affects a person's ability to communicate and interact with others. Individuals with ASD may have difficulty with social interactions, language development, and repetitive behaviors.

It's important to note that learning disabilities can manifest differently in each individual and may vary in severity. Understanding the different types of learning disabilities can help identify challenges and develop appropriate interventions and accommodations to support individuals with learning disabilities.

Challenges Faced by Individual's with Learning Disabilities

Individuals with learning disabilities face several challenges in their academic and personal lives. They may struggle with basic literacy and numeracy skills and face difficulty in following lectures, taking notes, and completing assignments. They may experience anxiety and low self-esteem due to the frustration of not being able to learn at the same pace as their peers. Learning disabilities can also affect an individual's social and emotional development, making it difficult to engage in social interactions and relationships. The lack of proper educational resources and support systems can further exacerbate the challenges faced by individuals with learning disabilities.

Learning disabilities can have a significant impact on academic development, affecting a student's ability to learn, communicate, and participate in academic activities. Some common ways that learning disabilities can impact academic development are:

Difficulties in Reading, Writing, and Math skills: Learning disabilities can make it challenging for students to acquire foundational skills in reading, writing, and math. Students with reading disabilities may struggle with phonics, comprehension, and vocabulary. Students with writing disabilities may find it hard to organize their thoughts and express themselves effectively in written form. Students with math disabilities may struggle with basic math concepts, such as number sense, operations, and problem-solving.

Challenges in Learning and Memorizing Information: Learning disabilities can also impact a student's ability to learn and remember new information. Students may have difficulty with working memory, processing speed, and recall. This can make it difficult for them to follow lectures, take notes, and study effectively.

Problems with Organizing and Completing Tasks: Learning disabilities can also affect a student's ability to plan, organize, and complete tasks. Students may have difficulty with time management, prioritization, and task initiation. This can lead to missed deadlines, incomplete assignments, and lower grades.

Struggles in Following Directions and Paying Attention: Learning disabilities can make it challenging for students to follow directions and stay focused on tasks. Students may have difficulty with attention, focus, and impulse control. This can make it difficult for them to stay on task, participate in class discussions, and engage with academic material.

Overall, learning disabilities can have a significant impact on academic development, affecting a student's ability to acquire new knowledge, participate in academic activities, and achieve academic success. It's essential for educators and parents to understand these challenges and provide the necessary support and accommodations to help students with learning disabilities succeed academically.

Implications of NEP 2020 for Individuals with Learning Disabilities

The NEP 2020 has several implications for individuals with learning disabilities. While the aim of the policy is to provide equitable, inclusive education for all, individuals with learning disabilities may face unique challenges in implementing the policy.

One of the primary challenges that individuals with learning disabilities may face is the implementations of the foundational literacy and numeracy program. This program is designed to ensure that every child achieves basic literacy and numeracy skills, which may be challenging for individuals with learning disabilities. Furthermore, the NEP 2020 emphasizes the use of technology in education, which may not be accessible to all individuals with learning disabilities.

The NEP 2020 has the potential to create a more inclusive and accessible education system for individuals with learning disabilities. However, there are several drawbacks that may affect this population. For example, the lack of qualified educators who specialize in learning disabilities can make it challenging to implement the policy effectively. Additionally, the large- scale implementation of policy changes can be overwhelming for those with learning disabilities who require more individualized lesson plans and support systems.

To ensure that individuals with learning disabilities achieve academic success under the NEP 2020, modifications need to be made to the policy. For example, additional support systems need to be put in place to assist individuals with learning disabilities in achieving basic literacy and numeracy skills, additionally, teacher training programs should cover the needs of individuals with learning disabilities, and qualified educators should be hired to cater to this population. The NEP 2020 should also emphasize the importance of individualized lesson plans to support the diverse learning disabilities.

Conclusion

In conclusion, this paper has explored the implications of NEP 2020 for individuals with learning disabilities. The finding of this paper highlight the importance of creating an inclusive and accessible education system that caters to the diverse learning needs of all students including those with learning disabilities. While the NEP 2020 has the potential to achieve this goal, there are challenges and areas that need modification to ensure that individuals with learning disabilities achieve academic success.

To ensure that NEP 2020 benefit everyone, policymakers should put in place support systems to assist individuals with learning disabilities with learning disabilities in achieving basic literacy and numeracy skills. Educators should be provided with training programs that cover the needs of individuals with learning disabilities and should be hired to cater to this population the NEP 2020 should emphasize the importance of individualized lesson plans and the use of assistive technology to support the diverse learning needs of all students.

In conclusion, the success of NEP 2020 in ensuring that individuals with learning disabilities achieve academic success will require a concerted effort by policymakers, educators, and the larger community. Together, we can build an inclusive education system that caters to the diverse learning needs of all students, regardless of their abilities.

References

Anandakrishnan, A. (2010). *Accountability and Transparency in University Governance*. University News, 48 (45), 18-23.

Government of India (2020). *National Education Policy 2020.* https://www.mhrd.gov.in/sites/upload_files/mhrd/files/NEP_Final_En glis_0.pdf, MHRD, New Delhi.

Jayaram, N. (1993). *Language Question in Higher Education: Trends and Issues*. Higher Education, Vol. 26, 93-114.

Ministry of Human Resource Development (MHRD 2019). *All India Survey of Higher Education*. Department of Higher Education, Government of India, New Delhi.

Varghese, N. V. (2021). *Directions of Change in Higher Education: From Massification to Universalization*. In Chattopadhyay, Saumen, Simon Marginson and N. V. Varghese (Eds.) *Changing Higher Education in India*. London, Bloomsbury Academic, 23-46.

5. Legal Education Through Window of NEP 2020: An Analysis

Dr. Harsha Suryawanshi

Introduction

Education is an important facet of civilization. In India, education can be classified as pre-primary, primary, elementary, and secondary education, followed by higher education. Further higher education can be categorized as traditional and professional education. Professional education aims to shape professionals after successful completion of professional education. Legal education is also categorized as professional education. Legal education is defined as 'a science which imparts to students' knowledge of certain principles and provisions of law to enable them to enter the legal profession'. Legal education thus, according to Law Commission is a science meaning principles proved by practice time to time. Legal education in simple words can be defined as successfully studying prescribed number of courses/subjects to practice as lawyer/advocate, interchangeably legal profession. As regards to legal profession, Justice Krishna Iyer says, Profession of law is a noble calling and the members of legal profession occupy a very high status.' Legal profession is also known as social engineering signifying that laws are used as means to shape society and regulate people's behaviour. Legal education is professional education regulated under the Advocate Act, 1961 through statutory body Bar Council of India. Unlike traditional programs that are governed by University Grants Commission, UGC in short, legal education is primarily regulated by Bar Council of India with the aid of UGC.

Importance of Legal Education

The State shall secure that the operation of the legal system promotes justice, on a basis of equal opportunity, and shall, in particular, provide free legal aid, by suitable legislation or schemes or in any other way, to ensure that opportunities for securing justice are not denied to any citizen by reason of economic or other disabilities. To provide legal aid, legal professionals are essential and these legal professionals are output of legal education.

Legal aid is essential as it is cardinal principle of jurisprudence that mistake of law is no excuse and law expects that everyone knows law of the land. Hence, to acquaint people with law of land, legal education is necessary.

In order to enable the State free legal aid and guarantee speedy trial, a vast number of persons trained in law are essential. This is possible only if adequate number of law colleges with proper infrastructure including expertise law teachers and staff are established to deal with the situation in an appropriate manner as held in State of Maharashtra vs. Manubhai Pragaji Vashi.

Lack of legal knowledge may make just claims and rights of people meaningless as held in Bhopal Gas Leak Disaster Case. Thus, lack of legal knowledge defeats ultimately objectives of law.

Highlights of NEP 2020 in View of Higher Education

The NEP highlights fundamental principles that shall guide the education system and educational institutions and these are summerised by UGC in Curriculum and Credit Framework for UG Programmes.
Transformative initiatives in higher education:

Introducing holistic and multidisciplinary undergraduate education that would help develop all capacities of human beings and ultimately rigorous specialization in chosen field of learning.

Flexible curricular Structures-Besides rigorous specialization in a subjects or subjects, students shall be allowed flexibility in course options in context of multidisciplinary study.

Undergraduate degree programmes of either 3 or 4-year duration with multiple entry and exit points and re-entry options and credit system. The degree programme shall have periodical certifications as below:

A UG certificate after completing 1 year (2 semesters) of study in the chosen fields of study and securing 40 credits.

A UG diploma after 2 years (4 semesters) of study and on securing 80 credits.

A bachelor's degree after a 3- year (6 semesters) programme of study and securing 120 credits.

A 4-year bachelor's degree (honours) after eight semesters programme of study and if student completes rigorous research project in his/her major areas of study in the 4th year of a bachelor's degree, it shall be honour with research and securing 160 credits.

NEP prefers 4-years bachelor's programme as it provides opportunity to experience full range of holistic and multidisciplinary education along with chosen areas of major and minor choices.

Regulation of Professional Education

Professional degree is an advanced education designed to prepare you to work in a specific field such as medical or law. In India, professional education prior to NEP 2020 was regulated by various regulatory authorities such as medical education by Medical Council of India, Pharmacy by Pharmacy Council of India, engineering and technical education by AICTE while legal education by Bar Council of India. The Supreme Court accepted need of Bar Council of India to regulate legal education in India across all law colleges across the country in view of fact that obtaining degree of law is pre-requisite for enrolment with Bar Council of India.

Role of Bar Council of India in Legal Education

The Bar Council of India, statutory body constituted under the Advocates Act, 1961 is responsible to promote legal education and lay down standards of such education in consultation with Universities in India imparting such education and the State Bar Councils. Similarly, the Bar Council of India is also empowered to prescribe standards of legal education to be observed by Universities in India and for inspection of Universities for that purpose. In accordance with its role, the BCI has prescribed Rules of Legal Education from time to time. At present the Universities are governed by   BCI Legal Education Rules, 2019. The BCI Legal Education Rules, 2019 prescribes:
Standards of professional legal education.
Recognition of degree in law.
Courses to be taught for programme in law.
Structure of semester system.

Admission and eligibility criteria for admission to law programmes.

NEP 2020 vis-à-vis BCI Regulation, 2019

Main thrust areas that are studied in the present research paper in perspective of NEP 2020 and BCI Regulation, 2019 are as below-
1.   Multiple Entry and Exit
2.   Multidisciplinary context
3.   Open and Distance Learning (ODL) and online education
4.   Academic Bank of Credit

Multiple Entry and Exit: NEP 2020 through credit structure permits multiple entry and exit points. At every exit point in academic programmes qualifications such as certificate, diploma, degree is organized in a series of levels. Undergraduate Certificate after exit after completion of two semesters of four-year Multidisciplinary UG Programme, undergraduate diploma after exit after four semesters or two years of Multidisciplinary UG Programme and bachelor's degree after exit after six semesters of minimum 120 credits. The intention under NEP 2020 in this regard is commendable as it recognizes time spent in any programme. A student can resume the Programme and continue the degree programme. Similarly, a student after acquiring requisite number of credits can join a Programme and allows lateral entry.

However, BCI does not recognise any certificate or diploma as professional programme of law mandates degree only. BCI strictly prohibits lateral entry.

Multidisciplinary Context: The NEP 2020 envisages imaginative and flexible curricular structures with multiple entry and exit options, to enable the creative combinations of disciplinary areas for study in multidisciplinary context (including vocational courses) thus, removing the currently prevalent rigid boundaries and creating new possibilities for life-long learning. For effective implementation of multidisciplinary four-year degree programme, the curriculum is required to be more flexible, with greater choices of credits across different streams.

However, in the context of legal education, BCI permits flexibility for integrated five years programme and not for three years programme.

Even though the Report is for four-year degree programme, it refers to legal education also.

Open and Distance Learning (ODL) and online education: NEP 2020 also focuses on open and distance learning. The NEP's vision includes key changes in current system and it includes:

9.3 (i) increased access, equity and inclusion through a range of measures, including greater opportunities for outstanding public education; scholarships by private/philanthropic universities for disadvantaged and underprivileged students; online education, and Open Distance Learning (ODL); and all infrastructure and learning materials accessible and available to learners with disabilities.

However, BCI expects classroom teaching and learning and nowhere in its Rules prescribes for open distance as well as online learning.

Academic Bank of Credit: The NEP prescribes that an Academic Bank of Credit (ABC) shall be established which would digitally store the academic credits earned from various recognized HEIs so that the degrees from an HEI can be awarded taking into account credits earned... However, the BCI does not prescribe such accumulation and transfer of credits. However, this provision of NEP might help legal education institutions for non-law courses.

Conclusion

The Supreme Court of India has accepted need and importance of Bar Council of India in legal education. Qualification and attributes of legal professional can be decided by BCI being regulatory authority and it can ultimately lay down standards of legal education to the institutions imparting legal education. Hence, unless the BCI makes requisite changes in its Rules of Legal Education NEP 2020 application to legal education institutions shall not be meaningful and effective.

References

(1995)5 SCC 730

Art. 39 A, Constitution of India, 1950.

Bar Council of India vs. Aparna Basu Mallick AIR 1994 SC 1334

https://www.legalserviceindia.com/legal/article-76-legal-education-in-india.html. Accessed on 6th February 2024

https://www.researchgate.net/publication/228175797_'Social_Engineering_by_Roscoe_Pound'_Issues_in_Legal_and_Political_Philosophy#:~:text=Social%20engineering%20is%20based%20on,through%20the%20help%20of%20Law accessed on 6th February 2024

NEP 2020 p.no. 37

NEP 2020 Report on Structure and Curriculum of Four Year and Dual Multidisciplinary Degree Programme with Multiple Entry and Exit Options for Implementation in State Universities of Maharashtra, p. no. 17

NEP 2020 Report on Structure and Curriculum of Four Year and Dual Multidisciplinary Degree Programme with Multiple Entry and Exit Options for Implementation in State Universities of Maharashtra, p. no. 64

Report on Structure and Curriculum of Four Year and Dual Multidisciplinary Degree Programme with Multiple Entry and Exit Options for Implementation in State Universities of Maharashtra

Rule 13 Bar Council of India Part IV Rules of Legal Education 2019 at p. no. 13

S. 49(2)(d) The Advocates Act, 1961

S. 7(6) The Advocates Act, 1961

6. Exploring the Integration of Home Science Curriculum within the NEP Framework

Dr. Shilpa Deshpande

Introduction

Education is very important in life as it helps us improve our life at the personal and social level by helping us gain useful skills, knowledge and training. It is important for developing a good career thus enhancing our quality of life, it is helpful for developing one's confidence as well as overall well-being. The importance of education is also pronounced in areas of creativity and innovation. Education encourages thinking outside the box and experimenting with new ideas.

In the report, "Reimagining Our Futures Together: a New Social Contract for Education," UNESCO (2021) points out climate change, democratic backsliding, growing social inequality, and growing social fragmentation as the four key issues on which all countries must center their education systems. Agenda of one of the goals of sustainable development (given in 2015 adopted by all countries) seeks to ensure inclusive and equitable quality education and promote lifelong learning opportunities for all by the year 2030 (Joshi & Somani, 2021). NEP places more of an emphasis on the student's overall learning than it does on rote learning and dense content. It offers interdisciplinary and innovative curricula in subjects including art, craft, languages and cultures, and sports and fitness. The goal of the policy is to merge vocational education programs with regular education and do away with social rank hierarchy. The strategy also acknowledges the significance of soft skills as essential life abilities, including teamwork, communication, problem solving, decision making, and analytical thinking. It promoted learning through experience and skill development. The India Skills Report 2024 emphasizes the need for comprehensive collaboration and proactive actions to bridge the skill gap and prepare the workforce for the changing job market.

Home Science is both science and social science-art related multidisciplinary fields of study. Home Science education deals with all aspects of home and family management. It is both an art and science. It's an 'art' because it helps you manage your resources in a skillful manner, and it's a 'science' because it helps to improve family life by offering knowledge in the field.

History of Home science

The evolution of Home Science education in India can be traced through several milestones. The roots of Home Science education in India can be linked to the efforts of pioneers like Anandibai Gopalrao Joshi and Jnanadanandini Devi. Anandibai was one of the earliest Indian women to receive a medical degree in the United States in the late 19th century. Jnanadanandini Devi, the wife of Satyendranath Tagore, established the first school for women's education in 1902, which included courses in home management. The teaching of Home Science in India is not very old, between 1920 to 1940, under the British administration; it was introduced in schools and colleges as Domestic Science, Home Craft, and Domestic Economy. The Princely state of Baroda was one of the first to introduce Home science in secondary schools.

Lady Irwin College in Delhi, established in 1932, played a pivotal role in the formalization of Home Science education. It was founded by Lady Dorothy Irwin, the wife of the then Viceroy of India. The college became a pioneer in providing education in Home Science and related disciplines. After India gained independence in 1947, there was an increased recognition of the importance of women's education and empowerment. Home Science gained prominence as a subject that not only focused on domestic skills but also encompassed broader aspects of family welfare, nutrition, and child development.

Over the years, several universities in India started offering undergraduate and postgraduate programs in Home Science. With time, the Home Science curriculum diversified to offer specialized courses in various branches such as Food and Nutrition, Human Development, Textiles and Clothing, and Family Resource Management. This allowed students to focus on specific areas of interest within the broader discipline. The National Education Policy 2020 has further emphasized the importance of holistic education, including life skills and practical knowledge. Home Science aligns well with the goals of NEP, contributing to the development of well-rounded individuals.

Home Science education empowers you with the skills to improve every facet of your home life – food, clothing, health, childcare, personal finance, religion, culture, arts, home beautification, etc. It enables you to take better care of your family while helping you lead a more enriched life. Home Science with its new nomenclature of Family and Community Sciences is an interdisciplinary course encompassing variety of subjects with the result it covers all the branches of Home Science called Food Science & Nutrition, Food Service Management and Dietetics, Human Development & Family Studies, Resource Management, Textile & Clothing, Communication & Extension etc.

Scope and Opportunities

The National Education Policy (NEP) places a significant emphasis on skill development to prepare students for a rapidly changing and dynamic world. Home Science practical play a crucial role in this context by offering hands-on experiences that contribute to the acquisition of a diverse set of skills. The goal of NEP's integration of Home Science into the curriculum is to provide students with a more comprehensive and well-rounded education, equipping them for life beyond the classroom. The home science program's emphasis on experiential learning is in line with NEP's goal of fostering students' ability to think critically, solve problems, and communicate effectively. Home Science integrates a number of courses, such as biology, nutrition, extension, sociology, and management, to support NEP's emphasis on transdisciplinary learning. NEP acknowledges the value of both academic knowledge and life skills. This requirement is successfully met by home science, which focuses on everyday activities like family dynamics, cooking, nutrition, and cleaning textiles. It gives students the fundamental life skills they need, encouraging a deeper comprehension of the real-world applications of personal wellbeing and home management.

Skill Development: A vast array of practical skills pertaining to child development, family resource management, textile design, interior décor, nutrition, and food preparation are included in the field of home science.

Complementing the NEP's emphasis on skill-based education, home science integration offers students experiential learning opportunities that foster critical life skills. Home science projects frequently incorporate nutrition and cooking lessons, which helps students develop their culinary skills. Along with learning about the nutritional value of food, they also pick up useful skills like meal planning, cooking, and food preparation. Through hands-on textile activities, Home Science students can hone their sewing, garment creation, apparel designing and fabric care skills. These abilities are beneficial not just for one's own use but also for future employment prospects.

Resource Management: Planning and executing Home Science practical require effective time management. Students learn to organize tasks, adhere to timelines, and complete activities efficiently, developing a crucial skill applicable in various aspects of life. Some Home Science practical incorporate budgeting exercises for meals or managing household expenses. This instills financial literacy, teaching students how to responsibly manage resources, a skill crucial for independent living.

Critical Thinking and Problem-Solving: Home Science practical often present real-life scenarios related to household management, nutrition planning, or family dynamics. Engaging with these scenarios encourages students to think critically and devise practical solutions, enhancing problem-solving skills.

Communication and Community Engagement: Home science education encourages students to apply their knowledge and skills to address real-world issues and challenges facing their communities. By engaging in community-based projects related to nutrition, health promotion, and sustainable living, students develop a sense of social responsibility and civic engagement, in line with the NEP's emphasis on promoting active citizenship and community participation. Many Home Science practical involve group activities, discussions, and presentations. This cultivates effective communication skills, teamwork, and the ability to articulate ideas clearly—skills that are essential in both personal and professional settings.

Gender equality: Home science curriculum promotes gender equality by challenging traditional gender roles and stereotypes associated with domestic responsibilities. By providing both male and female students with opportunities to learn practical skills related to cooking, sewing, and household management, home science education contributes to gender sensitization and empowerment, aligning with the NEP's objectives of promoting gender equality and inclusivity in education.

Health, Hygiene and Well-being: Practical sessions in Home Science often cover hygiene and safety practices, instilling good habits that are applicable not only in the kitchen but also in various environments, promoting overall well-being. Home science education emphasizes nutrition, health, and hygiene, promoting healthy lifestyles and preventive healthcare practices among students. With the NEP's emphasis on holistic development and well-being, home science curriculum can play a crucial role in nurturing physical and mental health awareness from an early age.

Entrepreneurial Skills: Home Science practical can provide insights into entrepreneurial opportunities, such as event planning or culinary endeavors. This nurtures an entrepreneurial mindset, encouraging creativity and innovation. With the NEP's emphasis on promoting entrepreneurial skills and fostering innovation, home science offers opportunities for students to develop entrepreneurial mindsets and pursue career paths in diverse fields such as food technology, textile design, and interior decoration.

Challenges in implementation

In alignment with the NEP's vision, Home Science practical contribute to a well-rounded education that goes beyond theoretical knowledge. These practical experiences equip students with a diverse set of skills, fostering their holistic development and preparing them for the multifaceted challenges of the future. The field of Home Science, encompassing various aspects of home management, nutrition, textiles, and human development, plays a crucial role in shaping individuals' understanding and practice of domestic life. However, like any educational discipline, it faces several challenges in aligning with the goals and frameworks set forth by the National Education Policy (NEP). Here are some of the challenges encountered by Home Science curriculum in light of the NEP:

Perception and Awareness: Despite its practical relevance, Home Science is often perceived as a less prestigious or academically rigorous subject. This perception can lead to a lack of awareness among students, parents, and even educators about the importance and potential career opportunities associated with Home Science education. Addressing this challenge requires concerted efforts to raise awareness about the value of Home Science within the NEP's broader vision of holistic education and skill development.

Teacher Training and Capacity Building: The successful execution of the Home Science curriculum necessitates highly qualified teachers who can impart to their pupils both theoretical knowledge and practical abilities. But there might not be enough trained home science instructors, and current programs might not prepare them well enough to address the wide range of demands of students within the NEP framework. To solve this issue, funding for comprehensive teacher preparation programs and capacity-building projects is crucial.

Resource Allocation: Home Science education requires specialized resources, including well-equipped labs, demonstration kitchens, sewing machines, and childcare facilities for practical learning. However, resource allocation for these facilities may be inadequate, especially in under-resourced schools and educational institutions. Ensuring equitable access to these resources and infrastructure is crucial for effective implementation of the Home Science curriculum under the NEP.

Curriculum Relevance and Adaptability: The requirements and problems of a changing society, such as shifting family structures, eating habits, and lifestyle trends, must be taken into consideration in the design of the home science curriculum. Within the NEP's vision of dynamic and future-oriented education, it is imperative that the curriculum be sufficiently flexible and adaptive to meet these changes while upholding a solid foundation in fundamental principles. It can be difficult to smoothly incorporate home science concepts and abilities into the larger educational framework, especially in light of the NEP's emphasis on multidisciplinary and holistic education. Curriculum creators, instructors, and legislators must carefully prepare and collaborate in order to ensure congruence with learning objectives across grade levels and to coordinate with other subject areas.

Assessment and Evaluation: It can be difficult to create suitable assessment tools to gauge students' comprehension and skill in home science, especially when working within the competency-based education framework of the NEP. Conventional test formats might not be able to fully assess students' application of knowledge and practical abilities. Accurately evaluating students' learning outcomes in home science depends on developing alternative assessment methodologies, such as project-based assessments, practical demonstrations, and portfolio evaluations. While necessary, creating real assessment instruments that support the goals of home science education can be time-consuming.

Addressing these challenges requires collaborative efforts from policymakers, educators, curriculum developers, and other stakeholders to ensure the effective implementation of the policy.

Conclusion

In summary, Home Science plays a vital role in NEP by offering a multidisciplinary approach, fostering life skills, and promoting experiential learning. Overall, the integration of Home Science in the curriculum under NEP enhances the educational landscape by nurturing well-rounded individuals equipped for real-world challenges. Implementing the Home Science curriculum within the framework of the National Education Policy (NEP) poses several challenges that need to be addressed for its successful integration and execution.

References

AJITE (ISSN :2395-616X) Amity International Journal of Teacher Education (AIJTE), Volume 9, No.1. April 2023, P-116.
History of Home Economics
https://ischoolconnect.com/blog/the-importance-of-education-reasons-why-we-need-it/
https://sites.middlebury.edu/homeec/history-of-home economics/
https://www.amity.edu/aien/aijte/articles2023/9.%20A%20Study%20on %20the%20Role%20of%20NEP%202020_%20Skill%20Developmen t%20of%20Students.pdf
https://www.ugc.gov.in/pdfnews/0794736_LOCF-Home-Science-Final-Report.pdf

Joshi. J.; Somani.P.(2021). *Indian National Policy on Education.* Towards Excellence: An Indexed, Refereed & Peer Reviewed Journal of Higher Education, vol.13. Issue no. 1, page numbers: 453-460; https://hrdc.ujaratuniversity.ac.in/Uploads/EJournalDetail/30/1045/40.pdf

UNESCO. (2021f). *Rememberin Our Future Together: a new social contract for education.* UNITED NATIONS EDUCATION. https://unesdoc.unesco.org/ark:/48223/pf0000379707.locale=en

7. The Crucial Role of India's National Education Policy-2020 in Shaping the Present Era

Dr. Munjaji K. Rakhonde

Introduction

The National Education Policy-2020, approved by the Union Cabinet of India, brings forth a paradigm shift in the country's approach to education. This policy, which comes after a gap of 34 years, aims to address the challenges posed by the rapidly changing global and technological landscape. With a focus on fostering creativity, critical thinking, and a multidisciplinary approach, NEP-2020 envisions a future-ready education system.

Education is the cornerstone of societal progress, and its role in shaping the destiny of nations is unparalleled. Recognizing the imperative to adapt to the dynamic demands of the present era, India embarked on a transformative journey with the formulation and implementation of the National Education Policy-2020 (NEP-2020). After a hiatus of 34 years, this policy stands as a testament to the nation's commitment to fostering a robust, equitable, and forward-looking education system. The NEP-2020, approved by the Union Cabinet of India, is a comprehensive document that not only acknowledges the challenges posed by a rapidly changing global landscape but also charts a course to harness the opportunities presented by this evolution. At its core, the policy envisions an education system that goes beyond the traditional boundaries of rote learning, encouraging critical thinking, creativity, and a multidisciplinary approach. The foundations of NEP-2020 rest on the principles of accessibility, equity, quality, affordability, and accountability. The policy recognizes the diverse educational needs of a nation as vast and varied as India and seeks to create a system that caters to individual strengths and preferences. This review article aims to explore the significance of NEP-2020 in the current context, examining its potential impact on accessibility, pedagogical methods, skill development, and the overarching socio-economic development of the nation. In this context, it becomes imperative to delve into the key provisions and reforms outlined in NEP-2020, deciphering how they align with the present needs of the Indian education system. From reforming pedagogical methods to prioritizing skill development and ensuring inclusivity, the policy sets forth a comprehensive roadmap that aspires to equip the youth with the necessary tools to navigate the challenges of the 21st century. As we navigate through the various facets of NEP-2020, it becomes evident that the policy is not merely a regulatory framework but a visionary document that seeks to redefine the very essence of education in India. Through a critical analysis of its components and a discussion of potential implementation challenges, this review aims to shed light on the transformative potential of NEP-2020 and its role in shaping the future trajectory of education in India.

Foundations of NEP-2020: A Multifaceted Framework for Educational Transformation

The National Education Policy-2020 (NEP-2020) is built upon a robust set of foundational principles aimed at redefining the contours of India's education system. These foundational elements, carefully woven into the policy, lay the groundwork for a holistic, inclusive, and forward-looking approach. The following sections elucidate the key foundations of NEP-2020:

Accessibility: NEP-2020 prioritizes universal access to education, acknowledging the diverse socio-economic landscape of the country. The policy envisions an inclusive education system that reaches every nook and corner of the nation, ensuring that education becomes a right rather than a privilege. Strategies to achieve this include the establishment of schools in underrepresented areas, special provisions for children with disabilities, and initiatives to reduce dropout rates.

Equity: Recognizing the existing disparities in educational opportunities, NEP-2020 places a strong emphasis on equity. The policy strives to bridge the urban-rural and socio-economic divides by implementing measures such as scholarships for underprivileged students, setting up special education zones, and providing resources for schools in economically disadvantaged regions. By addressing these disparities, NEP-2020 aims to create a level playing field for all students.

Quality: Quality assurance is a cornerstone of NEP-2020, seeking to elevate the standard of education across the nation. The policy emphasizes the need for rigorous accreditation mechanisms, standardized assessments, and continuous teacher training. By focusing on quality, NEP-2020 aims to ensure that students receive an education that is not only accessible but also of high standards, preparing them for the challenges of the modern world.

Affordability: NEP-2020 addresses the financial barriers that often hinder access to education by promoting affordability. The policy explores innovative financing models, scholarship programs, and public-private partnerships to make education more economically viable for all segments of society. This emphasis on affordability aims to mitigate financial constraints and enhance the overall accessibility of education.

Accountability: To ensure effective implementation, NEP-2020 introduces measures to enhance accountability at various levels of the education system. This includes setting up autonomous bodies for accreditation, periodic evaluation of educational institutions, and a focus on outcome-based learning assessments. By instilling accountability, the policy aims to create a results-oriented education ecosystem that is responsive to the evolving needs of students and society.

The interplay of these foundational elements forms the bedrock of NEP-2020, reflecting a commitment to creating an education system that is not only accessible but also of high quality, equitable, affordable, and accountable. As India moves forward in the implementation of NEP-2020, these foundations serve as a guiding framework for transformative changes that seek to redefine the landscape of education in the country.

Reforming Pedagogical Methods: A Paradigm Shift in Learning Approaches

One of the central tenets of the National Education Policy-2020 (NEP-2020) in India is the substantial reformation of pedagogical methods. Recognizing the limitations of traditional rote-based learning and the evolving demands of the 21st century, the policy advocates for a comprehensive overhaul in teaching and learning approaches. The following details shed light on the key aspects of the pedagogical reforms outlined in NEP-2020:

Experiential Learning: NEP-2020 places a significant emphasis on shifting from conventional rote learning to experiential learning. The policy advocates for hands-on experiences, practical applications, and real-world problem-solving exercises. By incorporating experiential learning into the curriculum, students are expected to develop critical thinking skills, problem-solving abilities, and a deeper understanding of concepts through direct engagement with the subject matter.

Holistic Education: The policy encourages a holistic approach to education that goes beyond the narrow confines of academic subjects. It emphasizes the integration of co-curricular activities, sports, arts, and vocational education into the mainstream curriculum. This holistic education model aims to nurture the overall development of students, fostering creativity, leadership skills, and a well-rounded personality.

Multidisciplinary Approach: NEP-2020 seeks to break down the silos between academic disciplines by promoting a multidisciplinary approach. It encourages students to explore a diverse range of subjects, fostering a broader understanding of the interconnectedness of knowledge. The flexibility in choosing subjects allows students to pursue their interests, promoting a more personalized and engaging learning experience.

Flexible Curriculum and Choice-Based Credit System (CBCS): The policy introduces a flexible curriculum framework that enables students to choose subjects based on their interests and career aspirations. Additionally, the implementation of a Choice-Based Credit System (CBCS) allows students to accumulate credits at their own pace, facilitating a more learner-centric and personalized educational journey. This departure from a rigid curriculum structure aims to cater to the individual learning needs of students.

Integration of Technology: Recognizing the transformative potential of technology in education, NEP-2020 advocates for the widespread integration of digital tools and resources. The policy encourages the use of educational technology to enhance teaching methodologies, facilitate interactive learning experiences, and provide access to a vast repository of information. This integration aims to make learning more engaging, accessible, and aligned with the digital age.

Teacher Training and Professional Development: NEP-2020 emphasizes the continuous training and professional development of teachers to align with the reformed pedagogical methods. The policy recognizes the pivotal role of educators in implementing these changes and calls for extensive training programs to equip them with the skills needed to adopt innovative teaching practices. This focus on teacher development aims to ensure the successful implementation of the reformed pedagogical approaches.

By embracing these pedagogical reforms, NEP-2020 seeks to cultivate a learning environment that nurtures creativity, critical thinking, and practical skills. The aim is to produce graduates who are not only academically proficient but also well-prepared for the challenges of the dynamic and evolving global landscape. Through these transformative changes, NEP-2020 envisions a future-ready education system that empowers students to thrive in the complexities of the present era.

Skill Development and Vocational Education: Empowering India's Workforce for the 21st Century

The National Education Policy-2020 (NEP-2020) in India places a strong emphasis on skill development and vocational education as key components of the education system. Recognizing the evolving nature of the job market and the need for a skilled workforce, the policy outlines comprehensive measures to integrate skill development and vocational education into the mainstream education landscape. The following details elaborate on the key aspects of the skill development and vocational education reforms within NEP-2020:

Early Exposure to Vocational Education: NEP-2020 advocates for the introduction of vocational education at an early stage, starting from the secondary level of schooling. This early exposure is designed to provide students with a diverse set of skills and practical knowledge that aligns with their interests and aptitudes. By integrating vocational education into the school curriculum, the policy aims to create a foundation for students to make informed career choices.

Flexibility and Choice in Vocational Courses: The policy promotes flexibility by allowing students to choose vocational courses alongside conventional academic subjects. This choice is intended to cater to the varied interests and career aspirations of students. The diverse array of vocational courses spans sectors such as agriculture, health, technology, and trades, providing students with a wide spectrum of options to pursue based on their individual inclinations.

Internships and Apprenticeships: NEP-2020 underscores the importance of practical experience through internships and apprenticeships. It encourages collaboration between educational institutions and industry partners to facilitate real-world exposure for students. By engaging in hands-on learning experiences, students can bridge the gap between theoretical knowledge and practical application, enhancing their employability and readiness for the workforce.

Industry-Academia Collaboration: To ensure the relevance of vocational education to industry needs, NEP-2020 promotes increased collaboration between educational institutions and industries. This collaboration facilitates the development of curriculum and training programs that align with the skills demanded by the job market. By involving industry experts in the educational process, the policy aims to create a seamless transition from education to employment.

Recognition of Prior Learning (RPL): NEP-2020 recognizes the value of skills acquired through informal means or work experience. The policy introduces Recognition of Prior Learning (RPL), which allows individuals to receive academic credit for skills acquired outside the formal education system. This recognition acknowledges the diverse pathways individuals may take to acquire skills and promotes a more inclusive approach to skill development.

National Skills Qualifications Framework (NSQF): NEP-2020 aligns vocational education with the National Skills Qualifications Framework (NSQF), providing a standardized framework for the recognition and certification of skills. This alignment ensures that vocational qualifications are nationally recognized and comparable, enhancing the credibility and portability of skills acquired through vocational education.

Entrepreneurship Education: The policy recognizes the importance of fostering an entrepreneurial mindset among students. NEP-2020 encourages the integration of entrepreneurship education at all levels of schooling, empowering students to explore and pursue entrepreneurial ventures. This emphasis on entrepreneurship aims to create job creators rather than just job seekers.

Through these comprehensive measures, NEP-2020 envisions a vocational education system that not only equips students with practical skills but also instills in them the ability to adapt to a rapidly changing job market. By promoting a seamless integration of skill development and vocational education into the broader education landscape, the policy strives to create a workforce that is not only employable but also capable of driving innovation and contributing to the economic growth of the nation.

Ensuring Inclusivity and Quality Education: Pillars of India's National Education Policy-2020

The National Education Policy-2020 (NEP-2020) in India places a significant emphasis on ensuring inclusivity and quality education as fundamental principles for the transformation of the education system. This dual focus aims to address the diverse needs of all learners while raising the overall standard of education across the nation. The following details elaborate on the key aspects of ensuring inclusivity and quality education within NEP-2020:

Foundational Literacy and Numeracy: NEP-2020 recognizes the importance of building a strong foundation in literacy and numeracy skills. The policy emphasizes early childhood care and education, with a specific focus on foundational literacy and numeracy for all students by the end of Grade 3. Special programs and interventions are introduced to address learning gaps and ensure that every child acquires basic reading and mathematical abilities.

Reducing Dropout Rates and Enhancing Retention: To promote inclusivity, NEP-2020 addresses the issue of high dropout rates in schools. The policy aims to create an environment that encourages students to stay in school by providing support systems, including counseling services, scholarships, and flexible learning pathways. By focusing on retention, NEP-2020 strives to ensure that education reaches every segment of society, irrespective of socio-economic background.

Multilingualism and Cultural Inclusivity: NEP-2020 recognizes India's linguistic and cultural diversity and promotes a multilingual approach to education. The policy encourages the use of regional languages as the medium of instruction while also emphasizing the importance of learning three languages. This multilingual approach aims to make education more accessible and inclusive, respecting and preserving the cultural diversity of the country.

Special Education and Inclusive Classrooms: NEP-2020 underscores the need for inclusive education, ensuring that learners with disabilities are accommodated in mainstream classrooms. The policy advocates for the development of suitable teaching-learning material, assistive technologies, and teacher training programs to create a supportive environment for students with diverse learning needs. This inclusive approach aligns with the broader goal of leaving no child behind.

Quality Assurance through Accreditation: Quality education is a central theme in NEP-2020, and the policy introduces stringent quality assurance measures. It emphasizes the establishment of accreditation frameworks for schools and higher education institutions to maintain and improve educational standards. The accreditation process ensures that institutions adhere to predefined quality benchmarks, fostering a culture of continuous improvement.

Digital and Online Education for Inclusivity: In light of the technological advancements, NEP-2020 recognizes the potential of digital and online education in reaching learners in remote areas. The policy encourages the development of digital infrastructure and the creation of online content to make quality education accessible to students across geographical boundaries. This digital push aims to bridge the digital divide and ensure inclusivity in education.

Flexible Board Examinations: NEP-2020 introduces a flexible and multidimensional approach to board examinations. The policy allows students to choose subjects based on their interests and provides multiple opportunities for board examinations to reduce the stress associated with a singular high-stakes examination. This flexibility caters to diverse learning styles and ensures that students are not marginalized based on their performance in a single examination.

Teacher Training and Continuous Professional Development: Recognizing the pivotal role of teachers in delivering quality education, NEP-2020 emphasizes teacher training and continuous professional development. The policy introduces mechanisms to enhance the skills and pedagogical knowledge of teachers, ensuring that they are well-equipped to address the diverse needs of students and create an inclusive learning environment.

By integrating these measures, NEP-2020 envisions an education system that is not only inclusive but also of high quality. The policy seeks to create an environment where every learner, regardless of background or ability, has access to education that empowers them to reach their full potential. Through these initiatives, NEP-2020 aspires to foster a culture of learning that is equitable, diverse, and capable of meeting the evolving needs of a dynamic society.

Conclusion

India's National Education Policy-2020 is a comprehensive and forward-looking blueprint that addresses the evolving needs of the present era. By emphasizing inclusivity, flexibility, skill development, and quality assurance, the policy aims to create a robust education system that prepares students for the challenges of the 21st century. While implementation challenges may exist, the potential positive impact of NEP-2020 on India's socio-economic development is significant.

References

Agarwal, R. (2022). *Transforming Higher Education: A Review of India's National Education Policy 2020*. Journal of Educational Planning and Administration, 36(1), 1-17.

Aslam, M. (2021). *The National Education Policy 2020: A Critical Analysis*. Economic and Political Weekly, 56(40), 32-38.

Ministry of Education, Government of India. (2020). National Education Policy 2020.

NITI Aayog. (2021). School Education Quality Index 2019-20.

UNESCO. (2020). Global Education Monitoring Report 2020.

8. An approach to design and development of the Auditory Training App

S.N. Lokhande, P.U. Bhalchandra, S.R. Mekewad and S.D. Khamitkar

Background

The human hearing capacity varies from person to person, but on average, the audible range for humans is from about 20 Hz to 20,000 Hz (20 kHz). However, as we age, our ability to hear high-pitched sounds decreases, and many people over the age of 30 may struggle to hear frequencies above 15,000 Hz [1].

The Speech Banana is a common term used to describe the range of frequencies and intensities that are important for human speech understanding [2].

Hearing loss occurs in the ear but also affects our brain and how we interpret and understand sounds; especially speech sounds [1]. The use of hearings aids and cochlear implants help us to detect sounds easier but it is important to help re-train the brain to better understand sounds and make sense of the information sent through the devices.

Auditory training is the process of improving and refining one's ability to process and interpret auditory information, such as speech, music, and environmental sounds [3]. There are several potential benefits to auditory training, including: Improved communication skills, better academic performance, enhanced music perception, improved cognitive function, and enhanced quality of life.

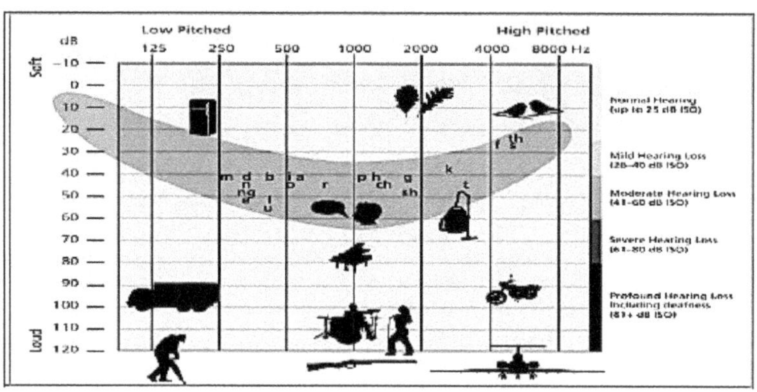

Figure 1: Speech Banana Audiogram

Due to shortage of audiologists affects fight against hearing loss. Smartphone hearing test applications are providing alternative tests in underserved areas that provide low-cost solutions that can result in early detection [4]. Equipment to screen for and diagnose hearing loss early enough particularly to prevent speech impairmentin children, is often too expensive for low income group family. Therefore, there is a need to develop practical, robust, and affordable mobile based application.

A mobile application, most commonly referred to as an app, is a type of application software designed to run on a mobile device, such as a Smartphone or tablet computer [9]. Mobile applications frequently serve to provide users with similar services to those accessed on PCs. Apps are generally small, individual software units with limited function.

Need for auditory training

Auditory training is the process of improving and refining one's ability to process and interpret auditory information, such as speech, music, and environmental sounds. This training is typically conducted through structured exercises designed to enhance listening skills, discriminate between sounds, and improve the ability to understand speech in difficult listening environments.

Due to shortage of audiologists affects fight against hearing loss. Smartphone hearing test applications are providing alternative tests in underserved areas that provide low-cost solutions that can result in early detection. This is particularly important in developing areas where audiology services are unavailable.

A Smartphone hearing test is easy to perform and can be self-administered at any time. The Smartphone based auditory training may be a supplement method in underserved areas to perform auditory training individuals.

There are several potential benefits to auditory training, including:

Improved communication skills: Auditory training can help individuals better understand speech in noisy or challenging listening environments, such as crowded restaurants, busy streets, or classrooms. This can lead to improved communication skills and better social interactions.

Better academic performance: Auditory training can also help students better understand and retain information presented in lectures or discussions, leading to improved academic performance.

Enhanced music perception: Auditory training can also help individuals better appreciate and enjoy music by improving their ability to discern musical elements such as pitch, rhythm, and timbre.

Improved cognitive function: Research suggests that auditory training may have broader cognitive benefits, such as improved memory, attention, and processing speed.

Enhanced quality of life: Finally, auditory training can improve the overall quality of life for individuals with hearing loss or other auditory processing disorders, by enabling them to better participate in social activities and communicate with others.

Auditory training can be a valuable tool for improving listening skills, enhancing communication abilities, and promoting cognitive and social well-being.

Review of Research and development in the subject

Related work in recent years, several studies investigated many aspects of mobile devices in audiometry, such as automated (Foulad et al. 2013; Thompson et al. 2015), screening (Swanepoel et al. 2014; Figueira et al. 2014), speech (Dewyer et al. 2018), tele-audiometry (Margolis et al. 2016; 2018) and game-based audiometry (Samelli et al. 2017; Yeung et al. 2013; 2015) using novel designed mobile applications. Particularly, studies of Yeung et al. (2013; 2015) and Thompson et al. (2015) validated automated audiometry using an iPad device equipped with a professional audiometric application, called "ShoeBOX Audiometry".

Research in mobile audiometry was recently reinforced by the comparative studies of Saliba et al. (2017) and Corry et al. (2017). Moreover, a preliminary study by Larrosa et al. (2015) discussed the development and evaluation of AudCal, a manual application for measuring hearing thresholds on iOS devices, although it was not intended to be a substitute for conventional audiometry. The cost of hearing aids can range from INR (Indian National Rupees) 15,000 to 2,50,000. This high cost makes these devices unaffordable for economically weaker section of the population.

According to WHO millions of people worldwide had moderate to profound bilateral hearing impairment. About 80% of these people lives in low- or middle-income countries.

Overview of the app for AT

Auditory training apps are designed to help users improve their ability to process and understand speech and other sounds. These apps can be useful for individuals with hearing loss, auditory processing disorder, or other conditions that affect auditory processing.
Some common features of auditory training apps include [9]:

Speech recognition exercises: These exercises involve listening to speech and then repeating it back or answering questions about what was said. They can help improve speech perception and understanding.

Sound discrimination exercises: These exercises involve listening to different sounds and identifying which ones are the same or different. They can help improve auditory discrimination skills.

Listening comprehension exercises: These exercises involve listening to longer passages of speech and then answering questions or summarizing what was said. They can help improve overall listening comprehension.

Adjustable difficulty levels: Many auditory training apps allow users to adjust the difficulty level of the exercises to match their current abilities. This can help ensure that the exercises are challenging but not too difficult.

Progress tracking: Many apps allow users to track their progress over time, so they can see how much they have improved and set goals for future training sessions.

Design process for developing the App

The design process for an app involves several stages, including ideation, prototyping, and user testing. Some of the key steps in designing an App [10] [11].

Ideation: The first step in designing an app is to generate ideas for what the app will do and how it will look.

Wireframing: The next step is to create wireframes or sketches of the app's user interface. presentation of the app's layout and structure, without any graphic design elements.

Prototyping: The team can move on to creating a prototype of the app. This might involve using tools like Adobe XD or Sketch to create a more detailed representation of the app's interface and user flow.

User Testing: User testing is a crucial part of the app design process. It involves recruiting users to try out the prototype and provide feedback on their experience. User testing helps the team identify usability issues and areas for improvement, and ensure that the app meets the needs of its intended audience.

Visual Design: This involves creating the visual elements of the app, including colour schemes, typography, and graphic design elements. The goal of the visual design is to create an attractive and engaging user interface that enhances the user experience.

Development: The final stage of app design is development, where the app is built using programming languages like Swift, Java, or React Native.

Features and functionality of the app

The features and functionality of the app will depend on its specific purpose, but here are some examples of potential features for an auditory training app:

AudiTrain app will include some of the basic auditory training exercises like:

Pure Tone Discrimination- In this group you gain practice in discriminating between different tones.

Environmental Sounds- In this group you can develop your ability to identify common everyday sounds.

Such as the sound of a bird chirping, a car horn blaring or a doorbell ringing. Being able to associate particular sounds with objects or events in your surroundings.

Male Female Recognition- In this group practice ability to distinguish between the voices of different speakers.

Vowel Recognition- In this group gain practice in telling the difference between vowel sounds. Training with many different words (such as cat, kit, cut, etc.) spoken by different speakers, able to identify vowel sounds.

Consonant Recognition- This group develops ability to recognize differences between consonant sounds. This helps in speech recognition, particular since different sounding consonants can have similar lip movements (for example, pat, bat, mat).

Word Discrimination- This group helps to listen to common words used in everyday speech, including words for animals, foods, colours and so on. Like other modules, repeating the words and comparing pronunciation to that of the speakers is an excellent way to practice.

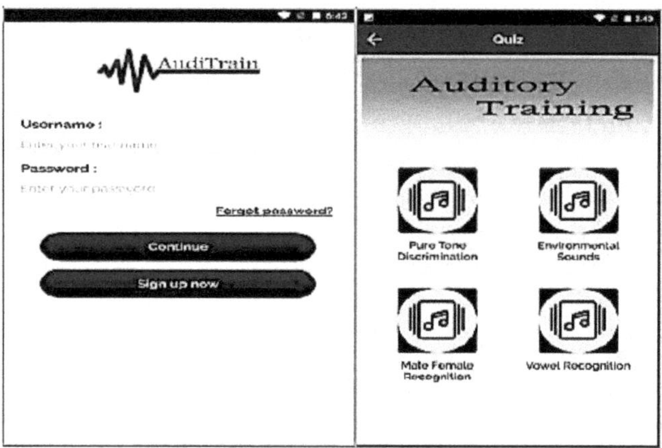

References

Corry, M., M. Sanders, and G. D. Searchfield. 2017. "*The Accuracy andReliability of an App-Based udiometer Using Consumer Headphones: pure Tone Audiometry in a Normal Hearing Group.*" InternationalJournal of Audiology 56 (9):706–710. doi:10.1080/14992027.2017.1321791.

Dewyer, N. A., P. Jiradejvong, J. Henderson Sabes, and C. J. Limb. "*Automated Smartphone Audiometry: Validation of a WordRecognition Test App.*" The Laryngoscope 128 (3) 2018. :707–712. doi:10.1002/lary.26638. doi:10.1097/AUD.0000000000000551. doi:10.1177/0194599813501461.

Foulad, A., P. Bui, and H. Djalilian. "*Automated Audiometry Using Apple iOS-Based Application. Technology.*" Otolaryngology- Head and Neck Surgery 149 (5) 2013:700–706.

Hearing Loss, written by Joanne Barker, Medically Reviewed by Brunilda Nazario, MD on September 26, 2020. (https://www.webmd.com/a-to-z-guides/hearing-loss-causes-symptoms-treatment)

Larrosa, F., J. Rama-Lopez, J. Benitez, J. M. Morales, A. Martinez, M. A. Ala~non, D. Arancibia-Tagle., et al. 2015. "*Development and Evaluation ofan Audiology App for iPhone/iPad Mobile Devices.*" ActatoLaryngological 135 (11):1119–1127. doi:10.3109/00016489.2015.1063786.

Margolis, R. H., G. Bratt, M. P. Feeney, M. C. Killion, and G. L. Saly. "*Home Hearing Test: WithinSubjects. Threshold Variability.*" Ear andHearing 39 (5) 2018:906–909.

Rohit Nambiar, Deval Karia, Kavyashree Venkatesh, "*A holistic approach to the design of hearing aids for children with hearing impairment in resource constrained setting*": 978-1-5386-5566-5/18/ IEEE, 2018.

Saliba, J., M. Al-Reefi, J. S. Carriere, N. Verma, C. Provencal, and J. M. Rappaport, "*Accuracy of MobileBased Audiometry in the Evaluation of Hearing Loss in Quiet and Noisy Environments.*" OtolaryngologyHead and Neck Surgery 156 (4):706–711, 2017, doi:10.1177/0194599816683663.

Samelli, A. G., C. M. Rabelo, S. G. Sanches, C. P. Aquino, and D. Gonzaga. "*Tablet-Based Hearing Screening Test.*" Telemedicine

Journal and e-Health: The Official Journal of the American Telemedicine Association 23 (9) 2017:747–752. doi:10.1089/tmj.2016.0253

ShekarMelati, KanisiusKaryono, Audio Detection (AudiTion): Asia-Pacific Conference on Computer Aided System Engineering (APCASE), 2014.

Yeung, J. C., S. Heley, Y. Beauregard, S. Champagne, and M. A. Bromwich, *"Self-Administered Hearing Loss Screening Using an Interactive, Tablet Play Audiometer with Ear Bud Headphones."* International JournalofPediatric Otorhinolaryngology 79 (8):1248–1252. doi:10.1016/j.ijporl.2015.05.021.

9. India's National Education Policy 2020 in Higher Eduction Institutions: A Perspective

Sachin M. Narangale

Multidisciplinary Education

National Education Policy (NEP) 2020 highlights Multidisciplinary education enabled with interconnections between different faculties. It seeks higher order thinking skills among students. The curriculum design has been recommended to be flexible so that students can choose from vast and different range of subjects across multi disciplines. A student of Arts discipline can choose from any other discipline like Sciences, Professional courses, humanities, etc. The objective is to remove the boundaries of disciplines.

Not only education but, research projects are also promoted to be interdisciplinary or multidisciplinary. Researches to solve real world problems may need the experts from different disciplines to work in collaboration. Practical based learning, on field learning, real world problem solving are key factors expected in the policy. Society inclusion is also expected in this policy. Healthy environment has to be facilitated for collaboration among industries and academic institutions to develop multi-disciplinary vocational training programs.

Nature of Higher Education Institutions

National Education Policy 2020 recommends separate institutions for separate objectives to reach excellence in all paradigms. Separate powers and tasks will be assigned to particular institutions. For example, research universities will be aimed with strong focus on innovation for real world problem solving through research. Overall nation's development will occur only if more number of researches are conducted and if more number of innovations are done for real world problem solving.

The primary mission of teaching Universities will be to provide high-quality education through teaching learning experiences for students. Teaching Universities can have affiliated colleges to provide education. Student engagement for learning outcomes and learning objectives will be facilitated and monitored by teaching Universities. Some institutions will have authority to provide degrees on their own, they will be called as autonomous degree granting colleges. These type of institutions will have powers to design their own syllabus, define teaching methods, develop industry-academia collaborations. The type of institutions may provide education depending upon the specialized needs of their region and industry expectations. If different Universities or colleges come together and initiate collaborative network, they will be termed as Cluster Universities. Sharing of resources, subject experts, knowledge, best practices, etc. are expected to happen in cluster Universities.

Ethics and Values in Higher Education

An overall development of an individual to have ethics, good behaviour, and integration, social and community responsibilities is the ultimate aim of National Education Policy 2020. The objective to include ethics and values in Higher Education is to prosper responsible citizens towards nation. The curriculum is expected to have ethics and values as compulsory components across all levels of higher education. Personality development of an individual to have moral values, value education, reasoning and taking decisions on social issues has to be integral part of education for all. Good leaders having characteristics honesty, integrity, empathy, cooperation, collaboration, responsibility are needed.

National Education Policy 2020 encourages higher education institutions to inculcate good leadership skills among students. Educators are the pioneers of any education system. Education without educators is not useful for anyone. In NEP 2020 educators are expected to follow ethical practices and professionalism in their interactions and demonstrations with students. Educators act as role-models. Students try to learn from the behaviour of educators. NEP 2020 promotes to accommodate ethical leadership within the institutions.

Promotion of Indian Art, Culture & Languages

National Education Policy 2020 promotes Indian Art, Culture & Languages significantly. Indian rich cultural heritage has to be preserved with a sense of pride among all citizens. The heritage has to be brought into the curriculum at all levels of education. Language should not be the barrier for education processes. Multilingual education and specifically education in mother tongue language has to be promoted.

Student-Centric Education

At the centre of National Education Policy 2020 is a student. All educational experiences, individual needs, interests of the student are important in NEP 2020. From this perspective, students are more involved in the academic activities. The assessment or evaluation will be based on competencies rather than memorization. Standardized testing has to be removed in NEP 2020. Students should be enabled to solve real world life problems, they should be able to apply their knowledge, they should be physically and mentally prepared to handle real life situations and act in a proper way in all circumstances.

Equity & Inclusion

National Education Policy 2020 expects a commitment from its stakeholders for provisioning equity to all learners. Quality education is for all, opportunities will be equal for all, personal and academic growth will be common for all are the keywords of equity in NEP 2020. NEP 2020 won't have any barriers in terms of socio-economic background, gender differences, caste wise, religious differences, etc. Social justice and equitable access have been emphasized in this policy. This policy focuses on commissioning of pre-schools in all communities including underserved areas. This policy emphasizes the innovative teaching methods to address learning gaps and ensure that all children will have the opportunity to acquire essential literacy and numeracy skills.

Curriculum & Syllabus Design

In National Education Policy 2020 recommendations are placed to promote Skill based education, flexible learning, multi-disciplinary education, learner centric education by developing a suitable curriculum.

This policy recommends a framework of syllabus to be shaped in pursuit of making India a developed nation. Essential skills such as critical thinking, real world problem-solving, digital education, collaborative education are expected in NEP 2020. The evaluation methods are going to be modified. Evaluations will be based on skills, understanding of concepts, task completion, field based assessment, etc. in this policy.

Findings and Recommendations

The NEP 2020 can be summarized as follows:
- This policy recognizes the importance of providing holistic education.
- Education will nurture the cognitive, social, emotional, and physical development.
- Rural and marginalized communities are having inadequate resources resulting in low access to education and quality of learning outcomes.
- Rapidly changing economy demands skill development and vocational education.
- NEP 2020 recommends foundational literacy and numeracy to ensure that all students acquire basic reading, writing, and arithmetic skills.
- Curricular reforms are proposed to make education more holistic, flexible, and interdisciplinary, with an emphasis on integrating 21st-century skills, arts, vocational education, and ethical values into the curriculum.
- Emphasizes to equip educators with the knowledge, skills, and pedagogical approaches needed to implement learner-centred and inclusive teaching practices.
- Promotes multilingualism, the mother tongue or local language.
- Recommends to conduct continuous and comprehensive evaluation methods.

References

National Education Policy 2020, Ministry of Human Resource Development, Government of India, https://www.education.gov.in/sites/upload_files/mhrd/files/NEP_Final_English_0.pdf.

National Education Policy 2020. https://nivh.gov.in/pdfdoc/nep_highlight.pdf.

National Education Policy, 2020. https://www.education.gov.in/sites/upload_files/mhrd/files/PIB1944287.pdf

Salient features of nep 2020: higher education. https://www.ugc.gov.in/pdfnews/5294663_Salient-Featuresofnep-Eng-merged.pdf.

10. NEP 2020 and Future of India

Dr. Deepak Subhash Waghmare

Introduction

The process of economic, social, and cultural development is built on education. A nation's education policy serves as a roadmap for its future development. Therefore, it is crucial that an education policy be future-oriented. An education policy represents the direction of a country's future development. The Government of India announced its first education policy of the 21st century. This new education policy comes after 34 years, since the 1984 policy. Currently, there is a lot of discussion surrounding this policy. It is widely accepted that education is a powerful tool for transforming lives. As society becomes more aware of the importance of education, we can all emphasize this point. After the central government formulated the policy, many states have adopted it. Some states have opposed it, while Maharashtra has begun the process of implementing it. The government has also made an announcement regarding this. However, the government faces a significant challenge in implementing this policy. The success or failure of a policy depends on the implementation of the policy by the workforce, considering its expected role. Therefore, if rapid change is to be brought about, it is necessary to have a capable and transformative workforce. This is why the policy suggests significant changes. Some new institutions will be established. To implement the policy, a large amount of funding is required. The availability of funds for this purpose is also equally important.

National Education Policy 2020

The National Education Policy 2020 was prepared under the chairmanship of eminent scientist Dr. D. K. Kasturiranjan. This policy considers five pillars: education for all, equality, quality, affordable education, and accountability. The policy takes a very comprehensive view. It also attempts to bring together our culture and the future. Emphasis is placed on making education enjoyable, as well as making it more life-oriented and employable. Implementation of the Policy While implementing the new education policy, the main focus is on how the policy will create a strong and supportive education system. While setting the goal of sustainable development, attention is also paid to how sustainable development can be achieved to a large extent. Therefore, it is necessary to pay maximum attention to the implementation of the policy.

According to the policy, the name of the Ministry of Human Resource Development has been changed to the Ministry of Education. The policy focuses not only on institution building but also on time-bound programs for quality improvement. This has raised expectations of success. If the implementation of the policy is effective, change will be certain. Otherwise, a situation of "another policy" may arise. Therefore, it is necessary to focus on implementation to make the policy most effective.

The new education policy for 2020 focuses on several key areas to improve the quality and accessibility of education in the country. Some of the key highlights of the policy include:

Universal access to education: The policy aims to ensure that every child in the country has access to quality education, regardless of their background or socio-economic status.

Curriculum reforms: The policy encourages a shift towards a more holistic and flexible curriculum that promotes critical thinking, creativity, and problem-solving skills. It also emphasizes the importance of vocational training and skill development to prepare students for the workforce.

Technology integration: The policy recognizes the importance of technology in education and aims to integrate it into the teaching and learning process to enhance the quality of education and make it more accessible to all.

Teacher training and development: The policy addresses the need for continuous professional development for teachers to ensure that they are equipped with the necessary skills and knowledge to deliver quality education to students.

Inclusive education: The policy emphasizes the need for inclusive education that caters to the needs of all students, including those with disabilities and special needs.

Assessment reforms: The policy aims to move away from rote learning and high-stakes examinations, and instead focus on continuous and comprehensive evaluation to assess students' learning and progress.

Overall, the new education policy for 2020 aims to bring about a significant transformation in the education system to ensure that every child has access to quality education and is equipped with the skills and knowledge needed to succeed in the 21st century.

The new education policy, unveiled in 2020, encompasses several key changes aimed at transforming the education system in the country. Some of the major highlights of the policy are as follows:

Holistic and flexible learning: The policy emphasizes a shift from rote learning to a more holistic and flexible approach to education, focusing on critical thinking, creativity, and problem-solving skills. This will involve a revamping of the curriculum to ensure a more well-rounded education for students.

Multidisciplinary approach: The policy encourages a multidisciplinary approach to education, allowing students to choose from a wide range of subjects and fields of study. This is aimed at fostering a broader understanding and appreciation of various disciplines.

Vocational and skill-based education: The policy underscores the importance of vocational training and skill development, aiming to provide students with practical skills and knowledge that are relevant to the current job market and industry needs.

Technology integration: The education policy emphasizes the integration of technology in the teaching and learning process, with a focus on digital literacy and the use of educational technology to enhance the quality of education.

Teacher training and professional development: The policy prioritizes the training and professional development of teachers, ensuring that they are equipped with the necessary skills and knowledge to deliver high-quality education to students.

Focus on early childhood education: The policy places a strong emphasis on early childhood education, recognizing its critical role in laying the foundation for lifelong learning and development.

Assessment reforms: The policy seeks to reform the assessment system, moving away from high-stakes examinations to a more continuous and comprehensive evaluation approach that provides a more accurate assessment of students' learning and progress.

Overall, the new education policy aims to bring about a fundamental transformation in the education system, with a focus on improving the quality, accessibility, and relevance of education for students across the country.

The new education policy 2020 comprises a comprehensive framework with multiple components aimed at transforming the education system in India. The key features and structure of the policy include:

Early Childhood Care and Education (ECCE): The policy emphasizes the importance of early childhood care and education, targeting children in the age group of 3-6 years, with a focus on the holistic development of young learners.

Foundational Literacy and Numeracy: The policy places a strong emphasis on foundational literacy and numeracy, aiming to ensure that every student achieves basic reading and mathematical skills by the end of Grade 3.

Curriculum and Pedagogy: The new policy advocates for a curriculum framework that is flexible, multidisciplinary, and promotes the integration of vocational education, critical thinking, and experiential learning. It encourages the use of innovative pedagogical methods and the incorporation of local and indigenous knowledge.

Assessment Reforms: The policy recommends a shift from rote learning to competency-based assessment, focusing on holistic development and continuous evaluation. It promotes formative assessments to provide timely feedback to students and teachers.

Vocational Education: The new education policy emphasizes the integration of vocational education and skills development from the early stages of schooling, aiming to equip students with practical skills and knowledge for various occupations.

Higher Education Reforms: The policy advocates for a multidisciplinary approach in higher education, offering greater flexibility in choosing subjects and multiple entry and exit options for degree programs. It also emphasizes the internationalization of higher education and the promotion of research and innovation.

Teacher Training and Professional Development: The policy emphasizes the continuous professional development of teachers, focusing on enhancing pedagogical skills, content knowledge, and the use of technology in teaching.

Technology Integration: The new policy highlights the integration of technology in education, promoting digital learning and the use of educational technology tools to enhance teaching and learning.

Governance and Financial Support: The policy includes recommendations for restructuring and strengthening educational governance at all levels, as well as increasing public investment in education to ensure equitable access and quality education for all.

Inclusive Education: The new education policy underscores the importance of inclusive education, catering to the diverse needs of all learners, including children with disabilities and those from marginalized backgrounds.

Overall, the structure of the new education policy 2020 reflects a comprehensive and holistic approach to revitalize the education system, with a focus on quality, equity, inclusiveness, and relevance to the needs of the 21st century.

While the new education policy 2020 has been hailed for its comprehensive approach and transformative vision, it also faces several criticisms and potential drawbacks, including:

Implementation Challenges: One of the primary criticisms of the new education policy is the potential difficulty in implementing its ambitious goals at the ground level. This includes challenges related to funding, infrastructure, teacher training, and administrative support.

Inequality in Access: Despite the policy's emphasis on equity, there are concerns that the implementation of the policy may continue to perpetuate existing disparities in access to quality education, particularly in rural and marginalized communities.

Overemphasis on Vocational Education: While integrating vocational education is important, there are concerns that an overemphasis on vocational skills might lead to a devaluation of academic education and limit the overall educational attainment of students.

Standardized Testing and Assessment: The policy's focus on competency-based assessment has raised concerns about the potential for increased standardized testing, which could lead to a narrow focus on test preparation and a lack of emphasis on holistic learning.

Language Policy: The policy recommends a three-language formula, emphasizing the importance of learning regional languages alongside Hindi and English. However, this has sparked controversy and concerns about the potential dilution of local cultural and linguistic identities.

Digital Divide: The policy's emphasis on technology integration in education may exacerbate the existing digital divide, particularly in rural and underprivileged communities where access to digital resources and connectivity is limited.

Autonomy and Regulation: Some critics argue that the policy's approach to granting autonomy to educational institutions may lead to challenges in maintaining quality standards and educational consistency across the system.

Teacher Preparedness: While the policy highlights the importance of teacher training and professional development, there are concerns about the readiness of educators to adapt to the proposed changes and the need for adequate support and resources.

Higher Education Reforms: The policy's multidisciplinary approach and flexibility in higher education have raised concerns about the potential fragmentation of academic disciplines and the quality of specialized education.

Lack of Stakeholder Engagement: Some critics argue that the development of the policy did not involve sufficient input from various stakeholders, including educators, parents, and students, leading to potential disconnect between the policy's goals and the on-the-ground realities.

It is important to address these potential drawbacks and challenges in a proactive manner to ensure that the new education policy can effectively bring about the intended positive transformation in the Indian education system.

The new education policy 2020 represents a comprehensive and ambitious roadmap for the transformation of the Indian education system. It aims to address critical issues such as access, equity, quality, and relevance while fostering a more holistic and flexible approach to learning and skill development.

Key findings and conclusions

Emphasis on Holistic Development: The policy places a strong emphasis on holistic development, recognizing the importance of cognitive, emotional, and physical development in shaping well-rounded individuals.

Flexibility and Multidisciplinary Approach: The policy introduces a flexible approach to education, allowing students to choose from a wide range of subjects and fostering a multidisciplinary approach to learning, which is crucial for adapting to the evolving needs of the modern world.

Integration of Vocational Education: By integrating vocational education into the mainstream curriculum, the policy aims to empower students with practical skills and knowledge to enhance their employability and entrepreneurial abilities.

Focus on Early Childhood Education: The policy underscores the importance of early childhood education as the foundation for lifelong learning and development, and provides strategies for improving access and quality in this area.

Technology Integration: The policy acknowledges the significance of technology in education and aims to leverage digital resources to enhance learning outcomes, improve access, and promote innovation in teaching and learning.

Redefining Assessment and Evaluation: The policy seeks to move away from rote learning and standardized testing, promoting a more comprehensive and competency-based assessment model that better reflects students' understanding and skills.

Inclusivity and Equity: The policy aims to address issues of social and economic equity by providing greater access to quality education, especially in underserved and marginalized communities.

Teacher Empowerment and Professional Development: Recognizing the pivotal role of teachers in shaping the education system, the policy emphasizes the need for continuous professional development and the creation of a supportive and empowering environment for educators.

Despite its transformative vision, the new education policy 2020 also faces challenges related to implementation, potential inequality in access, language policies, digital divide, and teacher preparedness, among others. It is crucial for policymakers and stakeholders to work collaboratively to address these challenges and ensure the effective implementation of the policy's objectives. In conclusion, the new education policy 2020 has the potential to significantly reshape the Indian education landscape, fostering a more inclusive, flexible, and relevant system that can better prepare students for the demands of the 21st century. However, the successful realization of these goals will require sustained commitment, resource allocation, and collaborative efforts to address the identified challenges and ensure that the benefits of the policy reach all segments of the society.

References

National Education Policy 2020, Ministry of Human Resource Development, Government of India, https://www.education.gov.in/sites/upload_files/mhrd/files/NEP_Final_English_0.pdf.

National Education Policy 2020. https://nivh.gov.in/pdfdoc/nep_highlight.pdf.

National Education Policy, 2020. https://www.education.gov.in/sites/upload_files/mhrd/files/PIB1944287.pdf

Salient features of nep 2020: higher education. https://www.ugc.gov.in/pdfnews/5294663_Salient-Featuresofnep-Eng-merged.pdf.

11. Building a Sustainable Future: NEP 2020's Role in Advancing the SDGs in Education

Dr. Suchita Suragihalli

In an era characterized by unprecedented global challenges, the imperative for sustainable development has never been more pressing. Central to this endeavor is the role of education, serving as both a means and an end in fostering societal progress. The United Nations Sustainable Development Goals (SDGs) symbolize a collective and global rallying cry, outlining a roadmap towards a brighter future for our planet and its inhabitants. Their primary aim is to achieve a significant transformation by 2030, addressing key issues like ending poverty, preserving the environment, and promoting prosperity for everyone. These goals are not isolated; instead, they are interconnected and interdependent, forming a complex network of challenges and aspirations. Central to these objectives is the imperative of tackling poverty head-on, recognizing its crucial role in sustainable development. Additionally, the SDGs stress the importance of improving education worldwide, underscoring its pivotal role in societal progress.

The National Education Policy 2020 aims to completely revamp the education system, encompassing its regulations and governance. Its objective is to establish a new framework aligned with the ambitious objectives of 21st-century education, including SDG 4, while drawing upon India's cultural traditions and values. The National Education Policy 2020 places significant emphasis on nurturing the creative abilities of every individual. It is founded on the belief that education should not only enhance cognitive abilities - both basic skills like literacy and numeracy, and advanced skills like critical thinking and problem-solving - but also foster social, ethical, and emotional development.

The United Nations' Sustainable Development Goals (SDGs) provide a comprehensive framework for addressing multifaceted global issues, while the National Education Policy (NEP) serves as a blueprint for transforming education systems at the national level. The adoption of the

National Education Policy (NEP) is a significant milestone for Countries like India, striving to equip their citizens with the skills and knowledge necessary to navigate the complexities of the modern world. However, the alignment of NEP with SDGs offers a unique opportunity to not only enhance educational outcomes but also foster broader socio-economic development. This article delves into the intricate interplay between SDGs and NEP, exploring how their alignment can catalyze holistic development and drive meaningful change. It establishes a symbiotic relationship between NEP and SDGs, elucidating the potential for transformative change and inclusive growth. The aim of Goal 4 is not only to increase children's enrolment in the education system, but also to ensure that children, supported by competent educators and adequate school infrastructure, achieve adequate academic performance and positive outcomes (Dixit, 2023).

Interconnectedness of SDGs and NEP

The NEP, unveiled in 2020, aligns seamlessly with the principles and objectives laid out in SDG 4, forming a harmonious partnership that holds tremendous promise for the educational landscape in India (Haripriya & Prema, 2023). At the heart of both SDGs and NEP lies a shared commitment to equitable and inclusive development. SDG 4 specifically targets quality education, aiming to ensure inclusive and equitable access to education for all. Similarly, NEP emphasizes the principles of equity, inclusion, and quality in education, with a focus on holistic development and lifelong learning. By aligning with SDG 4, NEP recognizes education as a fundamental driver of sustainable development, acknowledging its pivotal role in shaping future generations and fostering social progress.

NEP embodies a comprehensive vision for educational reform, emphasizing holistic learning, flexibility, and innovation. Its core principles resonate with the objectives outlined in the 2030 Agenda for Sustainable Development, encapsulated by the 17 SDGs. From ensuring inclusive and equitable quality education (SDG 4) to promoting gender equality (SDG 5) and fostering sustainable cities and communities (SDG 11), the SDGs provide a framework for addressing multifaceted challenges confronting societies worldwide. By aligning NEP with

SDGs, nations can harness the synergies between educational advancements and sustainable development imperatives. The synergy between SDGs and NEP extends beyond the realm of education. NEP encompasses broader developmental objectives, such as promoting environmental sustainability, fostering innovation and entrepreneurship, and advancing social cohesion. These objectives resonate with various other SDGs, ranging from environmental conservation - SDGs13 – Climate Action, 14 – Life below Water, 15 – Life on Land, to economic empowerment in the form of SDGs 1 – No poverty, 8 – Decent work and Economic growth, 9 – Industry, innovation and infrastructure. More importantly, these objectives are also connected to SDGs relating to social inclusion, SDGs 5 – Gender equality, 10 – Reduced inequalities and 16 – Peace, Justice and Strong Institutions. Thus, NEP serves as a channel for realizing a myriad of sustainable development objectives, transcending the boundaries of traditional education policy. It also helps to ensure that education is aligned with global development goals, promoting sustainable development, and contributing to the achievement of the SDGs (Radha & Arumugam, 2023).

Key Areas of Convergence

Several key areas of convergence between SDGs and NEP merit attention. Firstly, both frameworks emphasize the importance of inclusive and equitable access to education, irrespective of socio-economic background, gender, or geographic location. NEP's emphasis on universalization of early childhood care and education, inclusive education, and leveraging technology resonates with SDG 4's mandate to ensure inclusive and equitable quality education for all. It aligns with SDG 4.2, which aims to ensure that all girls and boys have access to quality early childhood development, care, and pre-primary education. One of the primary ways in which the NEP aligns with SDG 5 is through its advocacy for the removal of gender biases in educational materials (Haripriya & Prema, 2023). For years, textbooks and curricula have propagated gender inequalities through discriminatory and stereotypical content. The NEP aims to address this issue by promoting an inclusive and gender-sensitive learning atmosphere. In doing so, it moves closer to achieving the objective of SDG 5, which is to eliminate harmful stereotypes and biases. By prioritizing marginalized communities, addressing disparities in educational access, and fostering a culture of lifelong learning, NEP lays the groundwork for realizing SDG 4's transformative potential.

Secondly, both SDGs and NEP underscore the significance of quality education in fostering sustainable development. NEP's emphasis on holistic and multidisciplinary learning, as well as the integration of vocational education and skill development, resonates with SDG 4.7, which calls for ensuring that all learners acquire the knowledge and skills needed to promote sustainable development. Moreover, NEP's focus on vocational education and skill development aligns with SDG 8's goal of promoting sustained, inclusive, and sustainable economic growth, employment, and decent work for all, thereby nurturing human capital essential for sustainable development.

Furthermore, NEP's emphasis on environmental literacy and sustainability aligns with several environmental SDGs, such as SDG 4.7 (quality education), SDG 6 (clean water and sanitation), SDG 7 (affordable and clean energy), and SDG 13 (climate action). By integrating environmental education across curricula and promoting eco-friendly practices within educational institutions, NEP contributes to building a more environmentally conscious and resilient society.

Fostering Global Citizenship and Collaboration

As nations navigate interconnected global challenges, fostering a sense of global citizenship and collaboration becomes imperative. The convergence of NEP and SDGs presents a unique opportunity to catalyze community empowerment and foster inclusive societies. By aligning educational policies with sustainable development imperatives, nations can nurture a generation of empowered individuals capable of driving positive change within their communities. NEP's emphasis on multilingualism, cultural exchange, and global outreach cultivates a generation of empathetic and culturally competent individuals capable of engaging with diverse perspectives. By promoting international cooperation in education, research, and innovation, NEP facilitates cross-border collaborations essential for advancing SDGs at a global scale. NEP's emphasis on experiential learning, community engagement, and civic education lays the groundwork for fostering active citizenship and social responsibility. Through partnerships with local stakeholders, civil society organizations, and businesses, educational institutions can leverage their resources to address community needs and contribute to SDG implementation at the grassroots level. Through interdisciplinary approaches, service-learning initiatives, and community-based projects, educators can foster meaningful connections between learners and their communities, fostering a sense of belonging and collective responsibility. In addition, NEP's emphasis on ethics, values, and social-emotional learning fosters a sense of shared humanity and collective responsibility, underpinning SDG 16th goal of promoting peaceful and inclusive societies for sustainable development.

Holistic and inclusive communities are characterized by diversity, equity, and social cohesion, where every individual has the opportunity to thrive. NEP plays a pivotal role in fostering such communities by nurturing the holistic development of individuals and promoting values of empathy, respect, and inclusion. By prioritizing community engagement, service learning, and civic education, NEP cultivates a sense of belonging and collective responsibility among learners, laying the groundwork for inclusive communities aligned with SDG 11's vision of sustainable cities and communities. Moreover, NEP's emphasis on digital literacy and technology integration facilitates access to information and empowers marginalized communities, bridging the digital divide and fostering inclusive development.

Empowering Youth for Sustainable Development

Youth empowerment lies at the heart of both NEP and SDGs, recognizing the pivotal role of young people as agents of change. NEP's emphasis on experiential learning, critical thinking, and creativity nurtures a generation equipped to tackle complex challenges and contribute meaningfully to society. By integrating sustainability education across curricula, NEP fosters a sense of environmental stewardship and social responsibility among learners, aligning with SDG 12's call for sustainable consumption and production patterns. Furthermore, NEP's provisions for promoting research and innovation create pathways for youth-driven solutions to pressing sustainability issues, catalysing progress towards multiple SDGs.

Education serves as a powerful medium for achieving the SDGs, empowering individuals with the knowledge and agency to address pressing sustainability challenges. NEP's alignment with SDGs amplifies the impact of education in advancing sustainable development agendas. By integrating sustainability education across curricula, NEP fosters a culture of environmental stewardship, social responsibility, and global citizenship. Through interdisciplinary approaches and project-based learning, NEP equips learners with the skills to innovate and implement solutions aligned with SDG targets. Furthermore, NEP's emphasis on vocational education and skill development aligns with SDG 8's goal of promoting inclusive and sustainable economic growth, contributing to the creation of resilient and prosperous communities.

Lifelong Learning and Integration of Indigenous Knowledge

NEP emphasizes the importance of lifelong learning, recognizing that education is not confined to formal schooling but extends throughout one's life. It recognizes the importance of lifelong learning and skill development to adapt to the changing demands of the modern economy. SDG 9 aims to promote innovation and build resilient infrastructure, while the NEP 2020 emphasizes the need for developing an entrepreneurial mindset among learners (Radha & Arumugam, 2023). Through initiatives such as vocational education, adult literacy programs, and continuous professional development for educators, NEP supports SDG 4's objective of ensuring inclusive and equitable quality education for all throughout their lives. This aligns with SDG 4's emphasis on promoting lifelong learning opportunities for all, enabling individuals to acquire new skills and adapt to changing socio-economic environments.

NEP acknowledges the importance of indigenous knowledge systems and cultural diversity in education. By incorporating indigenous perspectives, languages, and cultural practices into educational curricula, NEP contributes to SDG 4's objective of promoting inclusive and culturally relevant education while also supporting SDG 10's goal of reducing inequalities by valuing and preserving diverse cultural heritage. By making both school and college education more comprehensive, flexible, and appropriate to the needs of the 21st century, NEP 2020, which is associated with the 2030 Agenda for Sustainable Development (SD), intends to transform India into a dynamic knowledge society and worldwide knowledge superpower (Patil, 2022).

Challenges

Challenges to achieving the education-related Sustainable Development Goals (SDG 4) are multifaceted and often interconnected with broader socio-economic and political factors. The NEP paves the path to deal with these challenges to a certain extent.

Inequality in Access: Disparities in access to education persist globally, with marginalized groups, including girls, children from rural areas, ethnic minorities, and those with disabilities, facing significant barriers to enrolment and retention. Economic inequalities, discriminatory practices, and lack of infrastructure exacerbate these disparities, hindering progress towards achieving universal primary and secondary education (SDG 4.1). The NEP, the Right to Education and other educational policies have created a more inclusive environment for such groups.

Quality of Education: While access to education has expanded, concerns remain regarding the quality and relevance of education provided. Poor infrastructure, overcrowded classrooms, inadequate teacher training, and outdated curricula contribute to low learning outcomes. Addressing these challenges is crucial for achieving SDG 4.2, which aims to ensure that all learners acquire the knowledge and skills needed to promote sustainable development.

Teacher Shortages and Quality: The shortage of qualified teachers, particularly in remote and rural areas, poses a significant obstacle to achieving SDG 4. Teachers are essential for delivering quality education and fostering inclusive learning environments. However, many countries struggle to attract, retain, and adequately train teachers, resulting in a lack of quality instruction and support for students. The NEP has provided for improving of teacher training standards, their professional standards and the support systems made available to them.

Conflict, Crisis, and Displacement: Armed conflict, natural disasters, and humanitarian crises disrupt education systems, leading to the closure of schools, displacement of students, and trauma among learners. Children living in conflict-affected areas are particularly vulnerable to being denied their right to education (SDG 4.3), perpetuating cycles of poverty and instability.

Lack of Funding and Resource Allocation: Insufficient investment in education, both domestically and internationally, undermines efforts to achieve SDG 4 targets. Many low-income countries allocate limited resources to education, prioritizing other sectors over schooling. Additionally, donor funding for education may be inconsistent or insufficient, hampering sustainable development efforts. The budget allocation for education has increased drastically in 2023-24from Rs. 59,503 crores to Rs. 68,805 crores which is whopping 15.6% increase. An additional Rs. 4000 crores have been made for Pradhan Mantri School for Rising India (PM-SHRI).

Technological and Digital Divides: The digital divide exacerbates inequalities in education, with disadvantaged communities lacking access to technology, internet connectivity, and digital literacy skills. The COVID-19 pandemic highlighted these disparities as schools shifted to remote learning, leaving many students behind due to a lack of access to online resources and devices. The NEP therefore, concentrates on development of Online Education, Digital Resources and content.

Cultural and Societal Norms: Deep-rooted cultural norms and societal attitudes, such as gender stereotypes and discriminatory practices, can hinder girls' education and perpetuate inequality. Addressing these challenges requires comprehensive approaches that challenge harmful beliefs and promote gender equality in education (SDG 4.5).

Data Collection and Monitoring: Limited data availability and inadequate monitoring mechanisms impede efforts to track progress towards SDG 4 targets accurately. Improving data collection systems and strengthening monitoring frameworks are essential for evidence-based policymaking and accountability in education.

Stakeholder Involvement in Policy Formulation: NEP development should involve input from diverse stakeholders, including community members, parents, educators, civil society organizations, and local leaders. By soliciting perspectives from various stakeholders, NEP can reflect the needs and aspirations of the community, ensuring that education policies are contextually relevant and responsive to local challenges and priorities.

Localizing Curriculum and Pedagogy: NEP can empower communities by allowing for the customization of curriculum and pedagogical approaches to reflect local contexts, languages, cultures, and values. By incorporating indigenous knowledge, community histories, and cultural practices into educational materials, NEP fosters a sense of ownership and relevance among learners, promoting active engagement and learning outcomes. By involving communities in the formulation and implementation of education policies, NEP can ensure that educational interventions are responsive, culturally relevant, and aligned with local aspirations and values.

The National Education Policy supplements the Sustainable Development Goals by providing a comprehensive framework for advancing quality education, promoting access and equity, fostering lifelong learning, integrating sustainable development themes, fostering innovation and research, promoting cultural and ethical values, and fostering partnerships and collaboration. By aligning educational policies and practices with the principles of sustainable development, NEP contributes to the realization of the broader agenda outlined in the SDGs.

In summary, the National Education Policy serves as a complementary framework to the Sustainable Development Goals, providing specific strategies and actions to advance educational outcomes, promote equity, and foster sustainable development. By aligning NEP with the SDGs, nations can maximize the impact of their educational policies and contribute effectively to the broader agenda of global development and progress.

References

Dixit M. (2023). *Education as the Sustainable Development Goal (SDG): NEP 2020*. In Dr. Pandey A. (Eds.), National Education Policy 2020: Transformation of Education System (pp. 53-61) https://www.researchgate.net/publication/371986129_Education_as_t he_Sustainable_Development_Goal_SDG_NEP_2020

Haripriya V. & Prema M. (2023). *Sustainable Development Goals and National Education Policy: A Synergistic Approach*. In Dr. Deep M. (Eds.), Impact of National Education Policy among Future Generation (pp. 517-526) https://www.researchgate.net/publication/375894620_SUSTAINABLE_DEVELOPMENT_GOALS_AND_NATIONAL_EDUCATION_POLICY_A_SYNERGISTICAPPROACH

Patil S. A. (2022). National Educational Policy 2020 - Heart of Sustainable Development Goals 2030. International Journal for Multidisciplinary Research (IJFMR) Volume 4, Issue 5 (pp 1-8)

Radha, L., & Arumugam, J. (2023). *Integrating the Sustainable Development Goals (SDGs) in the Curriculum and Strengthening Teacher Training Programs to Align with NEP 2020*. Shanlax International Journal of Education, 11(4), 63–68.

12. Adopting Multilingualism in NEP-2020: A Gateway of Opportunities in Teaching and Learning

Dr. Pandit B. Nirmal

Implementation of NEP-2020

The Government of India introduced the new National Education Policy - 2020 (NEP-2020) in July 2020 after the gap of 34 years of the last National Policy on Education 1986 (revised in 1992). Introducing the NEP-2020 in India is a paradigm shift in the entire education system in India. It provides a comprehensive, sustainable and reformative roadmap for the entire education system. It proves to be helpful for the new learning outcomes with changing world on the verge of globalization and technological advancement. The NEP-2020 proposes to transform our motherland into an equitable and vibrant knowledge society with the legacy of rich heritage of ancient Indian knowledge and be a global knowledge superpower. It also emphasizes the sustainable development of India and its each individual with creativity. It also proposes enrichment of Indian traditional knowledge, cultural heritage, national integrity and ethics and human values. In addition to it, the NEP-2020 suggests reforms in teaching-learning strategies like promotion of multilingualism in the teaching-learning process, synergy in curriculum, technology enhanced learning, multidisciplinary approach, respect for diversity, focus on life skills, and formative assessment. The promotion of multilingualism and power of language in NEP-2020 is focal point of the present research paper and how multilingualism proposes a paradigm shift in the entire education system and proves to be a gateway of opportunities for learners in their academic journey.

The NEP-2020 creates a vast scope for research on multilingualism in twenty first century. In this regard, Jean-Jacques Webder and Kristine Horner in their book 'Introducing multilingualism: A Social Approach' wrote, "Multilingualism is an exciting research topic to study because it is about people's use of language in the real world. It is people who code-switch and mix their languages, who set up fixed or flexible educational systems and who have certain ideas about how their societies should deal with multilingualism. And because human behaviors are so multi-faceted, there are always new developments in the study of multilingualism and new research areas opening up. (198)."

Multilingualism: Natural Phenomenon of Human Being

In order to comprehend the promotion of multilingualism in NEP-2020 and proposed ample opportunities in teaching and learning, it needs to define the term, multilingualism. "Multilingualism…should not be seen as a collection of 'languages' that a speaker controls, but rather as a complex of specific semiotic resources, some of which belong to a conventionally defined 'language', while others belong to another 'language'. The resources are concrete accents, language, varieties, registers, genres, modalities such as writing — ways of suing language in particular communicative settings and spheres of life, including the ideas people have about such ways of using their language ideologies" (Bloommaert, 2010, p.102). It is a natural phenomenon of day to day life. India is multilingual, multicultural, multi-religious and multi-ethnic country since time immemorial. "Multilingualism in India is a product of its history and a reflection of its diverse cultures" (Saraf, 2014, p.18). The Indian philosophy of 'udar charitanam tu vasudhaiva kutumbakam' which means those who are generous, the whole world is like their family is well known to the world. It preaches universal brotherhood and unity in diverse language, culture, religion and ethics. India is not united geographically but it is always united linguistically and culturally by maintaining linguistic diversity. Despite of several invasions on India by Portuguese, Dutch, French etc and long colonial rule of the British Raj, India is a land of unity of diversity where people of different linguistic groups live together. The various linguistic groups migrate from one part of the country to another part and interact with the peoples in their local languages. Unity in linguistic diversity has also become the strength of India. The interactions with invaders and migrants give birth to new languages and enrich the multilingualism in India. Sonu Saini in his research paper entitled 'Growing Multilingualism in India and Russia in the Light of Indigenous Languages' remarks that "Indian society has witnessed the multilingualism with the arrival or invasion by various ethnic groups and races since ancient times. The invasions through the history also have also witnessed migration from one society to other society, which exchanged the language, culture of each other. (p. 538)."

Promoting Multilingualism in NEP-2020

The implementation of NEP-2020 by the Government of India promotes multilingualism in the process of teaching and learning. In fact, multilingualism is a natural phenomenon of day to day life since the beginning of human history. The learning process especially acquisition, comprehension and conceptual knowledge of any subject is more natural and smooth in learners' home language/mother tongue. So the NEP-2020 suggests that the medium of instruction should be the mother tongue/home language/local language/regional language till at least Grade 5 and preferably till Grade 8 and beyond. This will be helpful to bridge the gap between the mother tongue of the learners and the medium of instruction and teaching. The NEP-2020 expects that, whenever possible, the home language or mother tongue will continue to be the language of communication between teachers and students. The importance of the medium of instruction, language of teaching-learning materials and language of communication is very aptly elaborated as, "Languages lie at the heart of teaching and learning processes. They shape the ways in which students communicate with each other, express themselves, engage with concepts, make sense their world, think and learn" (Halliday, 1993).

Multilingualism: A Gateway of Opportunities in Teaching and Learning

The NEP-2020 stresses the importance of multilingualism and power of language in the process of teaching-learning. As result, it creates ample opportunities for learners and teachers in their academic journey of acquisition and delivery of content. It appears that the New Education Policy (NEP) promotes multilingualism. It places a strong emphasis on creating a knowledge economy that is driven by skills and promotes using a multilingual framework to do it. The NEP emphasizes using the native tongue until at least Class 5, and preferably Class 8. It focuses on students becoming fluent in three languages, two of which must be their native tongues. The NEP-2020 encourages students to expose the different languages in the foundational stage because children acquire different languages extremely quickly between the ages of 2 and 8. With plenty of interactive conversation, early reading and subsequent writing in the mother tongue in the early years, as well as the development of skills for reading and writing in other languages, the students will study several Indian languages in an entertaining and interactive manner. There is an old and famous saying, "A man who knows two languages is equivalent to two men". This is due to the fact that a person who is multilingual will have a bigger social network and be able to integrate into a new environment without difficulty. Therefore, being multilingual gives a person a lot of autonomy and helps them fit in with a different culture and language (Saraf, 2014, 19). The NEP-2020 also suggests that students should be learned the Indian classical languages at least for two years for the betterment of their academic journey. In addition to it, students should be acquired the foreign languages like French, Korean, Thai, Japanese, German, Portuguese, Spanish, and Russian to broaden their knowledge of the world's cultures and to increase their mobility in according to their own interests and objectives (NEP 2020 Draft).

The NEP-2020 also encourages to the teachers to use a multilingual approach in order to enhance students' global knowledge and to avail ample opportunities in various fields of carrier. The teachers will be adopted various experiential and innovative teaching methods including extensive use of technology, educational apps, softwares and games. The teachers will use the cultural aspects of the languages such as theatre, films, storytelling, music, and poetry to enrich the teaching-learning process. In this regard, Helot remarks, "Understanding linguistic diversity in education means more than referring to plurality of linguistic systems or to the existence of different languages in society, it means analyzing the role of language(s) in education with a shift of perspective from the singular to the plural, or from a monoglossic to heteroglossic perspective stressing the plurality of uses within each language and across different language and across different languages" (Helot, 2012, p.126).

Integration of individuals from various cultural origins presents one of the largest obstacles to team management in today's corporate environment. Students will find it simpler to get along with people from other cultures and linguistic groups. An improvement in the pedagogy of teaching is what will, however, do the cause the most justice. It is necessary to change the way that languages are taught so that students may celebrate and engage with them through art, music, and culture. Only when a language is connected to culture and history can its actual nature be understood. Sadly, this is the area where our educational system has struggled.

Importance of Multilingualism in the Classroom

A significant amount of research has shown the advantages of multilingualism, and it is estimated that more than half of the world's population speaks two or more languages on a daily basis. However, the use of languages other than the language of teaching is still controversial in many classrooms today. Language policies that mandate the use of only one language for instruction are common, even at schools in nations that are traditionally regarded as multilingual. More recent research has shed light on the process of multilingualism and highlighted its many advantages. Contrary to what is commonly believed, languages are not kept independently in the brain, which is one of the main discoveries.

Considering the importance of multilingualism, it is harmful to force students to learn only one language in the classroom. Students feel free to participate in class discussions while using their mother tongue. They are unable to translate their knowledge into the language of instruction. Because a component of the students' cultural identity is not acknowledged, it may also have detrimental effects on their social and emotional development (Cathycollins).

Multilingualism: Enriching Languages, Culture and National Integrity

The promotion of multilingualism in NEP-2020 will be helpful to the students to empower themselves through the multiple languages to their own choice in the changing world. It shows flexibility in three language formula suggested by eight schedule of the constitution of India and no particular language will be imposed by any state of India. In spite of that, multilingualism will promote and preserve all Indian languages including classical, tribal and endangered languages. It will also strengthen the richness of different classical languages such as Marathi, Kanada, Telgu, Tamil, Malayalam, Sanskrit, Pali, Persian and others. With the help of multilingualism, Indian students should be aware of the richness of languages of their country. In all, promoting multilingualism is a quest to strengthen the richness of Indian languages, to reduce dropouts of students among rural and backward communities and to familiarize the students with India's diversity through the richness of different classical languages of our country.

The policy of multilingualism will create ample opportunities for students to participate in various activities based on the Indian languages under the 'Ek Bharat Shrestha Bharat' initiative. Students will discover the extraordinary similarity in scripts, grammatical structures, deep interrelationships, and diversity of the majority of the main Indian languages. Such activities would give students a sense of the unity and the rich cultural heritage and diversity of India. Shri. Dharmendra Pradhan, Minister of Education, Government of India, very aptly remarks, "NEP-2020 is a philosophy to realise the full human potential of India's demography, drive a culture of innovation and entrepreneurship as envisioned by the Prime Minister Shri Narendra Modi Ji, and create 'vishwa manavs' committed to global welfare in line with the ethos of 'Vasudhaiv Kutumbakam'. It is aimed at decolonising education and achieving aspirations, creating pride in our languages, culture and knowledge. We must bring in a transformative education system rooted in Indian values, thoughts and sense of service" (NEP 2020 Draft).

To sum up, multilingualism is a natural phenomenon of human life since time immemorial. The promotion of multilingualism in NEP-2020 provides a reformative roadmap for the entire education system in the 21st century. It will help students as well as teachers to transform India into a global superpower. It also proposes enrichment of Indian traditional knowledge, cultural heritage, national integrity and ethics and human values. The promotion of multilingualism also strengthens the richness of Indian languages, culture and knowledge. The policy of multilingualism proves to be a gateway opportunity for students as well as teachers in the process of teaching and learning. Students feel free to participate in class discussions by using their mother tongue and teachers easily deliver their knowledge to students with the help of multilingualism.

References

Bloomaert, Jean. (2010). *The Sociolinguistics of Globalization.* Cambridge University Press.

Cathycollins. (2018). *Multilingualism in the Classroom: Why and How it should be Encouraged.*

Halliday, M. A. K. (1993). *Towards a Language-based Theory of Learning.* Linguistics and Education, 5 (2), 93-116.

Helot, Christine. (2012). Linguistic Diversity and Education. Taylor & Francis.
https://modernlanguagesresearch.blogs.sas.ac.uk/2018/09/03/multilingualism-in-the-classroom-why-and-how-it-should-be-encouraged/
https://www.education.gov.in/sites/upload_files/mhrd/files/NEP_Final_English_0.pdf

Ministry of Human Resource Development. (2020). National Education Policy 2020.

Saini, Sonu. (2018). *Growing Multilingualism in India and Russia in the Light of Indigenous Languages.* Polylinguality and Transcultural Practices, 15 (4), 537—545. DOI 10.22363/2618-897X-2018-15-4-537-545.

Saraf, Ankit. (2014). *Language, Education and Society: Multilingualism in India.* Language and Language Teaching, 3 (2) Issue 6 July 2014, 18-21.

Webder, J. J., and K. Horner. (2012). *Introducing multilingualism: A Social Approach.* Routledge.

13. Research on Challenges in Data Analysis and Data Presentation

Anirudhha Pimpalgaonkar, Parag Bhalchandra & Gajanan Kurundkar

Introduction

Data is the "collection of unbiased details and figures that are methodically collected using observation, measurement, experimentation, or recording and used for reasoning, discussing or calculating in research" [1]. Data can also be defined as the "observations or measurements acquired using systematic approaches that can be numbers, words, or pictures and must be interpreted or analyzed to produce meaningful insights and conclusions in research" [2]. In today's world data has become more voluminous. Many companies gather huge datasets about their clients, suppliers, and other business matters; at the same time, sensors are becoming widely interconnected with physical objects including smartphones and cars which sense, produce, and transmit information.

Data analysis is a systematic approach that involves studying, cleansing, transforming, and modeling to discover useful information, draw conclusions, or support decision-making. Presentation of Data in Research Methodology is so vital that it varies depending on the method being used. For instance, giving out figures employed three kinds of procedures: observational studies, measurement interviews, and audio-taping which guarantee unbiasedness. This procedure starts with familiarizing oneself with the material to prepare for preliminary codes; then moving to concept search; clarifying these ideas until an expression arises. Figure 1 explains how data analysis works in the field of research.

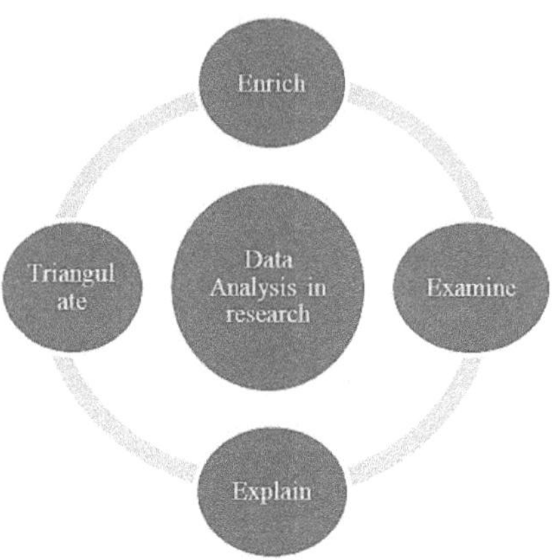

Figure 1. Data analysis in the field of research.

Significance of Data Presentation and Analysis in Research

The presentation of data is a crucial component of research methodology, which varies based on the chosen approach. The computation of data employed a combination of observational studies, assessment interviews, and recordings of sound to ensure a well-rounded and unbiased presentation. The process of data representation entails being acquainted therewith the data to develop preliminary codes, conducting a search for concepts, clarifying those topics, along ultimately producing an analysis. [3]. Data analysis is to transform unprocessed data, including factual data and opinions acquired through structured or unstructured preparation, observation, inspection, or studies into valuable knowledge. Consequently, this knowledge can then be employed to make informed decisions or to guarantee responsibility towards various stakeholders. Analyzing data can be conducted at several levels, encompassing individual projects, activities, working areas, and corporations. Data analysis is frequently promoted in social progress to facilitate collaborative growth within the community. Below, we will examine various categories of analyzing data.

Understanding Data Presentation for Data Analysis: Balancing Quantitative and Qualitative Approaches

The quantitative investigation becomes most beneficial whenever "answering questions of who, where how many, how much, and what is the relationship between specific variables" Nevertheless, quantitative research is not suitable for addressing inquiries related to causation and mechanisms [4]. Qualitative data is typically gathered near the unique issue, often using methods such as in-person observations or interviews. The local setting is taken into account and not disregarded [5].

Data Presentation

The representation of data serves as the fundamental basis for our shared insights into science, as the comprehension of readers regarding a data set is typically confined to the information that authors give in their articles. Figures play a crucial role as they frequently display the data that substantiate significant discoveries. Nevertheless, research published in both the Journal of the American Medical Association [6] as well as the British Medical Journal [7] gives convincing proof that scientists must make significant alterations to the types of numbers they employ. Typically, authors utilize figures to offer condensed statistical information, rather than presenting in-depth details about the data dispersion or displaying the complete dataset. Data can be displayed in three different formats:

Text - A text serves as the primary means of transmitting information, as it is employed to elucidate findings and patterns, as well as furnish contextual details. Data is primarily given in the form of phrases or sections.

Tabular form – Tables are a means of presenting information in a structured fashion using either numbers or words arranged in rows and columns. They have been in use for almost two millennia. The information displayed in a table can be simply comprehended by individuals who possess a satisfactory level of literacy. Tables are the optimal choice for displaying individual data and may effectively provide qualitative as well as quantitative data.

Graphical form - Graphs are a powerful tool for displaying extensive quantities of data and can be utilized instead of tables to showcase smaller data sets. It is crucial to select an appropriate graph layout that ensures clear comprehension of information by buyers and inspectors [8]. Figure 2 describes the types of data presentation.

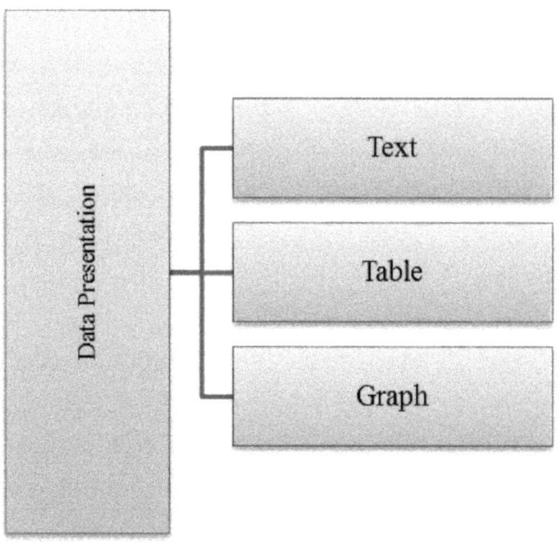

Figure 2: Types of Data Presentation

Current Research on Data Analysis and Presentation

Research being conducted today, on problems associated with data analysis and data presentation in education tells me that it is very important. A comprehensive examination reveals that researchers and authors have investigated certain pertinent studies in this domain.

Mbanaso et al., (2023) [9] study encompasses the subjects of data collecting, data display, and data evaluation. This study focuses on ways to gather data, which include research, analysis of pre-existing published or unpublished sets of data, observing, simulator and virtual twins, questionnaires, assessment interviews, including discussions in focus groups. An intriguing aspect of the present section is the segment that discusses the use of measuring scales in quantitative studies, encompassing nominative scales, scales of ordinals, interval scales, along scales of ratios. Elucidates fundamental aspects of qualitative research, encompassing the necessary prerequisites for ethical clearance. The study explores the significance of data visualizations as a crucial element in effectively presenting data. This includes many formats such as tabular forms, graphical forms, and visual charts like those produced by Atlas. Software for data analysis and interpretation.

Younas et al., (2022) [10] examined the techniques used for analyzing and presenting data in integrative analyses of nursing journals published between January - December the year 2019. This study examined 151 reviews, using summary tables for data extraction and a question-based process for synthesis. The methods were classified into four categories: not specific, inductive in that deductive, as well as framework-based. The majority of evaluations couldn't specifically specify their methodologies or employ inductive techniques. Fewer used deductive or framework-based methods. While narrative descriptions were common for presenting findings, several reviews included inventive techniques such as tables, diagrams of concepts, and word clusters. In summary, the findings provide a thorough comprehension of the many methods employed in data processing and presentation in integrated reviews.

Ma et al., (2020) [11] discussed the intricacies of data practice in digital history research, thus pointing out the need for a new interdisciplinary framework. This study employed a combination of interviews and questionnaires which went deep into ontological, flow-related, and more significant research issues. To ascertain these concerns, topics such as metadata guidelines, enabling effective data-sharing systems, and librarians' new roles in digital historical projects were also examined. In conclusion, it provided suggestions to improve data approaches for internet history that offered sensible advice about the field of library science.

Axon et al., (2020) [12] addressed this gap by studying attitudes towards sonification within Security operation centers (SOCs) as well as existing ways in which data has been represented. The researchers conducted online surveys (N=20) and interviews (N=21) with security practitioners from different SOCs. These included specifying contexts where sonification could be helpful for SOC practices; revealing potential limitations or complications; analyzing crucial imperatives for building sonification systems; and examining current visual presentation techniques of data. The findings shed light on possible benefits and problems associated with the implementation of sonification into SOC systems especially when it comes to supporting tasks such as anomaly detection like retroactive hunting). Those who took part realized how important it can be under conditions related to tracking boundaries or having multiple job responsibilities at once both inside and outside a SOC's scope.

Khowawisetsut et al., (2018) [13] highlighted the advances in flow cytometry technology that enabled phenotypic and functional characterization of different cell types. Despite its speed, objectivity, and quantification advantages, polychromatic flow cytometry poses difficulties in data analysis. The purpose of this communication was to enumerate some approaches for presenting and analyzing both univariate and multivariate datasets in flow cytometry. It dwells on the multi-parametric aspect of flow cytometry that has not only helped researchers to simultaneously analyze extensive populations of cells but also given a better understanding of complex systems such as the immune system.

Hu et al., (2014) [14] researched to complete a review of previous works and presented an elaborate tutorial on big data analytics platforms. The purpose was to give a general understanding of these platforms about those who are not experts in this area as well as enable advanced users to tailor their solutions. The study has opened with the definition of big data and the challenges faced by it. This was followed by a systematic organization that would break down large-scale data systems into four separate modules that were creating data, acquiring and storing data, and analysis of the same. Apart from that, different methodologies have been explored including Hadoop, which is widely used both academically and industrially. Finally, the authors provided an explicit guideline for evaluating major sets of data known as Big Data sets in addition to giving possible areas that need more studies later.

Kandel et al., (2012) [15] research sought to investigate the process of conducting data analysis in the presence of societal and organizational environments that are inherent to large corporations, as well as acknowledging the central position played by data analysts in a variety of organization functions. Despite many tools for analysis and visualization aimed at improving efficiency for analysts, there was little knowledge about how such an analysis occurs within an organizational setting. To fill this gap, researchers conducted informal interviews with 35 data analysts across 25 firms from various sectors. Using these interviews, they identified the enterprise analyst ecosystem while also documenting how certain organizational traits influence the analytical process. The study revealed typical obstacles hindering the implementation of graphical analytic tools in businesses. The authors dwelled upon creative aspects and potential new visual analytic studies emerging out of their findings.

Bertini et al., (2010) [16] based on the research goal of the study was to evaluate and analyze the combination of visualization with data extraction for effective knowledge discovery, drawing on human and machine strengths. A top-down bibliographical research methodology was used in the article to classify observed methodologies, determine current trends, outline deficiencies, as well as suggest possible subjects for future research. This study analysis considers the advantages and disadvantages of information visualization (InfoVis) as well as data extraction by studying how researchers in each field take advantage of techniques from others. In line with extracted patterns, potential extensions previously not recorded were suggested in the article. Eventually, this information helped to interrogate the process of discoveries by juxtaposing analytical procedures between information visualization and data extraction revealing new insights in improving human and machine capabilities alike. These thoughts led to considerations that yielded inquiries relevant to advancing visual analytics science.

Potter et al., (2010) [17] conducted a study on the problem of noting that the presentation of unclear data has become a challenge. In scientific datasets, no errors, checks, or confidence intervals could be seen and it was difficult to present them visually. The project was influenced by graphics data analysis to create graphic representations that display both the data values and important data qualities, such as uncertainties. A revised version of the classic box plot was developed, which includes a fresh hybrid summarized plot. This plot combines descriptive statistics to efficiently emphasize important characteristics of the data. Furthermore, a 2-dimensional distribution was introduced as a component of the summarized plot. Ultimately, the study presented an example of how these novel plots might be used to provide comprehensive summaries and in-depth analysis of the data distribution.

Conclusion

In conclusion, this review has brought to light the importance of analyzing and presenting data as aspects of research design. This study has explained how significant it is in displaying results appropriately. In addition, the study has also discussed the relationship between qualitative and quantitative approaches in analyzing data while noting that when doing research; one must use appropriate methods depending on the objectives being investigated. The study has further explored different styles through which information can be represented focusing mainly on their advantages and disadvantages. Lastly, this paper recognizes ongoing studies seeking solutions about educational issues such as dealing with difficulties linked with analyzing information or presenting statistics, etc., thereby underscoring a need for more exploration into this field.

References

Adler L. *Qualitative research of legal issues*. In: Schimmel D, ed. *Research That Makes a Difference: Complementary Methods for Examining Legal Issues in Education*, NOLPE Monograph Series; vol 56. NOLPE; 1996.

Axon, Louise. Bushra A. AlAhmadi, Jason RC Nurse. Michael Goldsmith, and Sadie Creese. "*Data presentation in security operations centers: exploring the potential for sonification to enhance existing practice*." Journal of Cybersecurity 6, No. 1 2020:tyaa004.

Bertini E, Lalanne D. *Investigating and reflecting on the integration of automatic data analysis and visualization in knowledge discovery*. ACM SIGKDD Explor Newsl. 2010;11(2):9-18. doi:10.1145/1809400.1809404.

Cooper RJ, Schriger DL, Close RJ. *Graphical literacy: the quality of graphs in a large-circulation journal*. Ann Emerg Med. 2002;40(3):317-322. doi:10.1067/mem.2002.127327, PubMed: 12192357.

Creswell JW, Creswell JD. *Research Design: Qualitative, Quantitative, and Mixed Methods Approaches*. 5th ed. SAGE Publications; 2017.

Hu H, Wen Y, Chua T-S, Li Xuelong. *Toward scalable systems for big data analytics: A technology tutorial*. IEEE Access. 2014;2:652-687. doi:10.1109/ACCESS.2014.2332453.

In J, Lee Sangseok. *Statistical data presentation*. Korean J Anesthesiol. 2017;70(3):267-276. doi:10.4097/kjae.2017.70.3.267.

Kandel S, Paepcke A, Hellerstein JM, Heer J. *Enterprise data analysis and visualization: an interview study*. IEEE Trans Vis Comput Graph. 2012;18(12):2917-2926. doi:10.1109/TVCG.2012.219.

Khowawisetsut L, Sukapirom K, Pattanapanyasat K. *Data analysis and presentation in flow cytometry*. Scienceasia. 2018;44S(1):19. doi:10.2306/scienceasia1513-1874.2018.44S.019.

Ma R, Xiao F. *Data practices in digital history*. Int J Digit Curation. 2020;15(1):21-21. doi:10.2218/ijdc.v15i1.597.

Mbanaso UcheM, Abrahams L, Okafor KC. *Data collection, presentation and analysis. In: Research Techniques for Computer Science, Information Systems and Cybersecurity*. Springer Nature Switzerland; 2023:115-138.

Miles MB, Huberman AM. *Qualitative Data Analysis: An Expanded Sourcebook*. 2nd ed. SAGE; 1994.

Ningi AI. *Data presentation in qualitative research: the outcomes of the pattern of ideas with the raw data*. Int J Qual Res. 2022;1(3):196-200. doi:10.47540/ijqr.v1i3.448.

Polit DF, Beck CT. *Nursing Research: Generating and Assessing Evidence for Nursing Practice*. 11th ed. Wolters Kluwer; 2021.

Potter K, Kniss J, Riesenfeld R, Johnson CR. *Visualizing summary statistics and uncertainty. In: Comput Graph Forum*. Blackwell Publishing Ltd. 2010;29(3):823-832. doi:10.1111/j.1467-8659.2009.01677.x.

Schriger DL, Sinha R, Schroter S, Liu PY, Altman DG. *From submission to publication: a retrospective review of the tables and figures in a cohort of randomized controlled trials submitted to the British Medical Journal* [journal]. Ann Emerg Med. 2006;48(6):e751-e721. doi:10.1016/j.annemergmed.2006.06.017, PubMed: 16978740.

Younas A, Shahzad S, Inayat S. *Data analysis and presentation in integrative reviews: A narrative review*. West J Nurs Res. 2022;44(12):1124-1133. doi:10.1177/01939459211030344.

14. The Influence of AI on English Language Teaching

Jyothi Gedela & Dr. Swati Bhise

Introduction

Around the world to be interconnected universally one needs to be an expert in the command of the English language as it's intrinsically important to upgrade one personality on all the different streams where everyone is brought under one roof to communicate. Especially the academicians, professionals, researchers, policymakers, and students. In the Global Community, one can easily communicate if the proficiency of the English Language is very good. It is a continuous process of demand for achieving the English Language skills among the explorers and the various approaches are always in trend as Technology advances. The inclusiveness of Artificial Intelligence (AI)has become a pivotal role in imbibing while Teaching English Language. It has been observed that the maximum English Teachers would come to terms with their students to learn to have practical knowledge outside the closed rooms of the classroom to upgrade their command of communicative competence.

Artificial Intelligence, distinguished through its potential to imitate human intelligence, massively developed in latest years, exploring various territories of society. In the pedagogy field, AI has been utilized exclusively as an assurance instrument to withstand and upgrade language teaching, specifically to the explorers of communication skills. In the procedure of language acquisition AI facilitates several learning techniques such as on immediate basis feedback, customizable assessments, and individualized content that dominates to improvise the individualized learning pathways. This draws attention upon the native learners who are unable to communicate and lag due to unresponsive feedback and no personal attention.

Method

This paper employs the calculated beginning to accumulate and investigate reliable findings regarding the part of Robotics in enhancing English dialect instruction such as Recognizing the Research objective by examining the part being played by intelligent retrieval in expanding English speech teaching for presentation abilities, primarily working towards learning skills such as speaking, listening, reading, and writing territory based on three perspectives of efficacy of AI-based tools, teaching associations, and moral's considerations.

Results and Discussion

The key findings from the book Artificial Intelligence and English language teaching: Preparing for the Future by Dr Adam Edmett et al that there is an intense Educational interest in AI in English language teaching.

Speaking and listening

"Other technologies used for improving speaking skills included using AI for speech recognition, adaptive learning, automatic speech analysis, and voice assistance." Dr. Adam Edmett (15).

Writing

"Another common use of AI in writing is the use of AI grammar checkers" (16).

Grammarly gave higher contributions in correcting their grammatical and helping with lexical. several tools were connected to correct their errors. Other tools such as Grammar checkers, writing assistants, translation tools, and pattern checkers acted as helping tools to formulate the proper sentences. Even Google Translate also supported many poor learners to produce essays with higher proficiency and greater presentation.

Reading

"The findings suggest that learners have opportunities to learn vocabulary and understand meaning via games beyond what a textbook or classroom can provide, by contextualising often decontextualised vocabulary." (16).

Several apps provide services to develop reading skills by including AI characters and including challenging navigation algorithms to create the surroundings energetic and occupied.

Discussions

In the paper Effects of Intelligent Tutoring Systems (ITS) on Personalized Learning (PL) by Yasar Akyuz has stated that the customized educational approach is applied according to the individual's IQ level, grasping power, adaptation, facilities, and added individual characteristics. The area of interest is important to keep up with the attention of the learners. With the inclusion of an Intelligent Tutoring System which assists in technological solutions through the medium of Artificial Intelligence, process control, and machine learning to produce instructional command on an individual basis. As it inculcates a learning environment where we witness a human teacher handling a student with close teaching interaction. It has been observed few research's are going on to handle with the challenges that they come across. Machine learning is capable of understanding the emotions of the students, their individual phases, and intellectual design to furnish customized learning results.

The paper Artificial intelligence technologies and applications for language learning and teaching by Jeong-Bae Son et al has highlighted the trends in the sector of AI and its contribution to language learning. Several applications such as computer-assisted language learning (CALL), natural language processing (NLP), data-driven learning (DDL), automated writing evaluation (AWE), computerized dynamic assessment (CDA), intelligent tutoring systems (ITSs), automatic speech recognition (ASR), and talkbot. They have stated that through the advancement of AI one can be liberated from the inside classroom learning, due to immediate feedback and adaptable studying surroundings. still after so many technological advancements many demerits have been raised and are under the research to analyze the uncertainties of AI in Emotions recognition and on AI instructor subordinate. But finally, lots of emphasis is laid upon future research and technical issues in pedagogy, and progress of AI, and the successive operation of AI.

From the paper, The Role Of Artificial Intelligence (AI) In Developing English Language Learner's Communication Skills by Rusmiyanto et al that there are several methods of AI need to be focused on the success of Knowledge Engineering in progressing English Language trainee's Verbal proficiency, didactic suggestions of Integrating AI in Language Learning and high principled thoughts in Machine learning-operate dialect study but still, we find Gaps and Future Directions in the adaptation of natural language processing in English dialect teaching, more work to be done in the area of best practices of neural network in dialect schooling surroundings, more focus toward be laid upon the Ethical structure under the consideration to prioritize the confidentiality, safe future, prejudice, and lucidity affairs in respect of structure as well execution of intelligent retrieval innovations in dialect education.

Challenges

For new technology there were always demerits that existed so here we have come across certain challenges which are under scrutiny such as:
1. Technology Breakdown which resulted in breakdown and loss of association.
2. Limited capabilities of certain apps reduced the interest in the requirement of the app due to its variation in capability, for example, Chatbot.
3. Fear of trust issue upon the AI 's functioning system and even being under the fear of losing the traditional environment of learning.
4. Standardized language and ideologies: it was found certain apps were not updated into Google translate as standardized apps for formatting purposes which were untouched due to their historical and political language boundaries.

Conclusion

AI is assured to have a greater impact on the English language teaching and learning, as the demand is increasing around the world. There is an intrinsic relationship between the rise in demand that directs towards the provision of supply of well-organized and profitable teaching methods and drawing attention towards the apps of AI. It has been stated that AI will withstand with the challenges of present scenario and satisfies the requirement of the society.

References

"artificial intelligence and English language teaching research" ... (n.d.-b). https://teachingenglish.britishcouncil.org/artificial-intelligence-and-english-language-teaching-research-british-council

Akyuz, Y. (2020). *Effects of intelligent tutoring systems (ITS) on personalized learning (PL)*. Creative Education, 11(06), 953–978. https://doi.org/10.4236/ce.2020.116069

Son, J.-B., Ružić, N. K., & Philpott, A. (2023, September 15). *Artificial Intelligence Technologies and applications for language learning and teaching*. De Gruyter. https://www.degruyter.com/document/doi/10.1515/jccall-2023-0015/html

Rusmiyanto, R., Huriati, N., Fitriani, N., Tyas, N. K., Rofi'i, A., & Sari, M. N. (2023). *The role of Artificial Intelligence (AI) in developing English language learner's communication skills*. Journal on Education, 6(1), 750–757. https://doi.org/10.31004/joe.v6i1.2990

15. NEP 2020: The Role of Language and Literature

Kailas Baburao Tidke & Dr. Ramesh Bhanudas Jaybhaye

Introduction

Language is a form of expression. It is an integral part of human beings. Man is a social animal. Without the use of language, there would be no communication among each other. It is an effective medium of expressing thoughts, ideas, knowledge, and information from one person to another. Culture evolves through language. India is a treasure house of culture developed over a thousand years ago in the form of art, linguistic expressions, traditions, literature and heritage. In this process, culture developed through language which created a huge literary base. This literary foundation of society assists us in knowing the evolution of its language and culture since its inception. National Education policy primarily focuses on the development of culture through language and literature. No culture can be sustained without the preservation of its language and literature. The various regional languages like Sanskrit, Marathi, Bengali, Telugu, Gujarati, Punjabi, Rajasthani, Tamil and many more contributed a lot to developing culture and literature in the respective context. The NEP also concentrates on the dissemination of ancient literature to inculcate moral and ethical values in modern society.

Importance of the topic

To know the role of language and literature under the light of NEP 2020 while promoting the Indian Languages.

The National Education Policy 2020 amply focuses on the promotion of the Indian languages and mother tongue irrespective of their status. The issue of language will be dealt with in great detail both at schools and higher education levels as a medium of instruction, as well as an independent discipline.

Thus, language of course is basically connected with Literature, art and culture. Different languages have their approach to seeing the world through different lenses. Therefore, the structure of language determines a native speaker's awareness and understanding. Especially, language influences the way people of their respective culture speak with the members of family, authority, peers and strangers; and influence the tone of the conversation. Literature plays a crucial role in preserving and promoting native languages and culture. Unfortunately, Indian native languages didn't get due attention and care as a result the country lost the existence of over 220 languages in the past 50 years. If we try to understand the diversified linguistic culture, we come to know that, there are certain unscripted languages that are unrecognized till the present time. Therefore, NEP insists the various institutions like schools and colleges integrate teaching and learning of Indian languages at all levels to preserve the rich culture of these languages.

To promote and preserve the Language and the literature and create a vibrant space in the education system, it is essential to provide high-quality learning material print as well as virtual learning in these languages like; textbooks, videos, plays, novels, magazines etc. English is a global language enriched with a huge literature of the world. Facilitating various learning resources and materials carried out by countries around the world created the dominant space of language in the global setup. However, Indian languages didn't get that much attention and recognition due to the attraction of Western culture and scope for employment. Teaching language in the Indian Education system is given a secondary place. Due to the advancement of technology and global employment opportunities, English is considered an important language. It is a business language. Everyone who wants to learn English has a specific intention be it for employment or business advancement. We cannot preserve our art, culture and literature merely by learning English. We have to be careful in giving education in native languages to protect the Indian ethos and customs. NEP envisages the future of art, language and literature through standard guidelines:

"All curriculum and pedagogy, from the foundational stage onwards, will be redesigned to be strongly rooted in the Indian and local context and ethos in terms of culture, traditions, heritage, customs, language, philosophy, geography, ancient and contemporary knowledge, societal and scientific needs, indigenous and traditional ways of learning etc. – to ensure that education is maximally relatable, relevant, interesting and effective for our students. Stories, arts, games, sports, examples, problems, etc. will be chosen as much as possible to be rooted in the Indian and local geographic context. Ideas, abstractions, and creativity will indeed best flourish when learning is thus rooted."

NEP 2020 emphasizes teaching not only vocabulary, grammar and literature but also interaction to develop communication skills among students at all levels. Learning Language and Literature should not only be a part of academics, it should be used to create the ability to converse and interact in the language. It is essential to adopt the three languages formula in schools and teaching-learning in bilingual and trilingual formats for better understanding. NEP also focuses on the skills development of teachers to enhance learning outcomes and make learning enjoyable. Skilled language teachers are scarce in India. It could be the reason for putting language in the secondary place. Secondly, all the courses and programs run by various educational institutions aim to provide professional education which is based on employment. Therefore, students somehow manage to get through it instead of getting exhaustive knowledge of language and literature. NEP 2020 Further states:

"The National Education Policy 2020 (NEP 2020) has emphasized the use of mother tongue or local language as the medium of instruction up to class- V while recommending its retention up to class-VIII and above. It recommends that all students learn three languages in school according to formula. The three languages they learn will be the choice of the students. "

The core idea behind the introduction of the English language as the chief medium of education was to integrate Western culture among Indians to bring stability to the British rule in India. It is a welcoming gesture for promoting regional languages and promoting cultural integration through language. It will help to gain the lost respect of the native languages and give a global platform to regional languages and literature. The policy further focuses on the empowerment of Indian ethos and best practices giving regional languages a global platform.

It must be noted that a need for the promotion of native languages by the Indian Government is to create awareness among students of all levels to learn Indian culture and ethos. But the facts and figures may vary. The real condition of the present age-long education system has drastically failed to promote the native languages of the nation. It is done for the self-satisfaction that, one knows his culture and possess proud of it. The policymakers' role in doing so is utterly ironical and doubtful. Many Indians are fluent in their mother tongue yet they are not habitual to write it properly. It is because the dominance and superiority of the English language tempered the Indian people. They believe that English is the language of imperials, which can pave the way to economic progress. This is not a denying fact that the most intelligent Indians prefer to pursue their higher studies abroad. Therefore, it becomes mandatory for them to adopt English as the language of communication and medium of learning. It is the window of global knowledge. Hence, language plays a crucial role in the academic as well as professional development in and across the country. On the contrary, the native or regional languages are considered subsidiaries of this race.

Conclusion

It is said that the whole world is a global village due to technological advancements and innovations. However, the National Education Policy 2020 emphasizes the promotion of Indian languages and literature to preserve the Indian culture and encourage speech. Even after the political independence higher education system in India is still dependent on a single language. Moreover, the limited number of individuals in India taste the fruit of true knowledge and the majority of the Indians are deprived of getting the benefit of it. The government shall make inclusive policies that help a common citizen to get easy access to education on all levels. NEP-2020 promotes an interdisciplinary approach to education. Language and literature act as bridges to connect different subjects and facilitate a comprehensive understanding of different concepts. Language fluency especially English, is considered essential for effective communication and employability.

References

Aithal, P. S., & Aithal, S. (2020). *Analysis of the Indian National Education Policy 2020 towards achieving its objectives.*

International Journal of Management, Technology, and Social Sciences, 5 (2), 19-41.

Arya Aarti, Jotania Piyush, Nanaware Rajkumar, *NEP 2020 - Reformation of Indian Education System*, Nexus Publication, Surat, First Edition, 2021

Dixit, R. K. (2021). *National Education Policy (NEP) 2020 - Opportunities and Challenges in Teacher Education* (Chapter-12, 120-129). Book-National Education Policy 2020: Meeting Sustainable Development Goals. HSRA Publications, Bangalore.

Dr. Singh, Jaba Kusum. *The Importance Of English Language Learning And Nep-2020*. An international Journal of Interdisciplinary studies volume V, issue-3

https://drc.casel.org/uploads/sites/3/2019/02/Equity-Social-and-Emotional-Learning-A-Cultural-Analysis.pdf

https://en.wikipedia.org/wiki/National_Education_Policy_2020

https://www.frontiersin.org/articles/10.3389/fpsyg.2021.732182/full

https://www.quora.com/There-are-3-languages-in-the-family-Is-it-safe-to-teach-our-future-kids-3-languages-from-the-moment-they-are-born

Mehrotra Dr. Dheeraj, NEP 2020- At a Glance for Educators, First Edition, 2021

National Education Policy 2020, Ministry of Education, Government of India, 2021Akyuz, Y. (2020). *Effects of intelligent tutoring systems (ITS) on personalized learning (PL)*. Creative Education, 11(06), 953–978. https://doi.org/10.4236/ce.2020.116069

Verma, Hemlata & Kumar, Adarsh (2021): *New Education Policy 2020 of India: A Theoretical Analysis. International Journal of Business and Management Research*. Vol. 9, Issue 3, 30th August, 2021

16. Achieving NEP 2020 Goal of Educational Equality through Artificial Intelligence: Opportunities and Challenges

Dhrumi Shah & Dr. Swati Bhise

Introduction

Educational inequality is a significant issue that needs to be addressed if global well-being, equality, and justice are to be achieved (Blanden, 2022). Moreover, in a socio-culturally diverse country like India, equality in education becomes a priority for policymakers, administrators, and educators (Kundu, 2014). Various measures undertaken to promote access to education and attain better socio-economic outcomes for the population include the Indian Constitution, making provision for compulsory and free education to children in the age group of 6 to 14 years a fundamental right, and the National Policy on Education (1986). Even the latest National Education Policy 2020 assigns importance to equal and inclusive education in school and higher education (MHRD, 2020). While such policies have increased school enrollment and adult literacy (Kundu, 2014), there still exist disparities in accessing and continuing education because of socio-economic differences, school environment, infrastructure, and quality of teaching, and other social, cultural, and traditional factors like gender, age, and ability (Tilak, 2002, as cited in Kundu, 2014).

The persistent educational inequality in India draws attention to the failure of past education-related policies to tackle inequality in a holistic way. NEP 2020 may also meet the same fate if a framework or solution that offers a wholesome solution is not formulated and implemented. Given the emphasis on the potential of artificial intelligence (AI) to accomplish inclusive and equal education in Sustainable Development Goals 2030 (UNESCO, 2023), incorporating AI in the context of the Indian educational milieu emerges as a lucrative and all-encompassing solution to achieve the NEP 2020 goals of inclusive and equal education.

Thus, the present study will explain the inequities and problems connected with the current education system in India and elaborate on how AI can be harnessed to address the problems. It will also consider the challenges involved in making AI-driven education in India a reality.

Indian Education: Inequities and Problems

The Indian education system is primarily plagued by two major issues: inequality of access and system inefficiencies (Arya & Yadav, 2020). While the former stems from socio-economic differences and traditional factors like gender, age, and ability, the latter stems from problems in the educational environment, infrastructure, and quality of teaching.

In considering socio-economic differences and traditional factors as contributors to access disparities, it is first important to understand the geographical, social, and economic diversity of the country. Because of the urban-rural dichotomy, there is a difference in the quality and quantity of educational institutions. In rural areas, there is a lack of up-to-date infrastructure, competent teachers, and modern educational resources. As a result, even those availing themselves of education in rural areas because of the education-supportive policies are unable to receive education and skills that are on par with those gained by urban learners. In addition to this, a majority of the population in rural areas is economically impoverished. This forces children to work and function as breadwinners for the family. Unable to dedicate time to gaining education, these children are trapped in unequal educational and economic outcomes because a lack of education also impacts their economic prospects. Moreover, the need to contribute to family income also results in high dropout rates, thereby negatively impacting the overall morale of the system. Further, the digital divide is another aspect of the urban-rural dichotomy. Although digitalization in India has improved access to technology and internet connectivity and encouraged online learning, many factions of the population in rural India do not have access to these services. This divide amplifies inequalities.

Gender discrimination is a significant traditional factor that contributes to educational inequalities. Due to cultural norms like early marriage, safety concerns, and preference of male child over female child, there are lower enrollment and higher dropout rates in girls.

Additionally, age-related and ability barriers also hinder educational opportunities in the country, as the educational system is not equipped to address issues of gaps in education, adult literacy, robust childhood education, and specialised education for the differently abled.

Along with this, the Indian education system suffers from poor infrastructure, discouraging learning environments, systems, and quality of teaching (Kumar, 2023). Many schools in urban areas are also not well-equipped with state-of-the-art mechanisms and continue to follow the rote learning system. Consequently, learners receive outdated education, which fails to make them employable in the long run. The poor quality of teaching because of unskilled and untrained teachers in the system also has a negative influence on education outcomes. Besides this, the standardised system of assessment also does not cater to the specific needs of individual learners, thus failing to address learner diversity.

Achieving Educational Equality through AI: Opportunities and Challenges

Harnessing AI can help address all the challenges discussed above. AI has the potential to transform the entire educational system and prove advantageous to educators, learners, administrators, and policymakers.

AI can help overcome the barriers to education posed by the urban-rural dichotomy by providing remote learning opportunities (Feng, 2023). The ability of AI to deliver customised content and offer virtual tutors and chatbots will help learners access education irrespective of their location and empower them. In providing education across the nation, AI will also eliminate the drawbacks of the traditional system concerning standardised instruction and assessment. Competent to analyse immense amounts of data, AI will give insights into patterns in students' preferences and their learning styles. This way, learners' interests, weaknesses, and strengths will be taken into account, real-time feedback will be made available to learners, and educational inclusivity will be fostered.

Moreso, AI will also be able to address the linguistic diversity of India and promote educational equality for differently abled learners and learners with special needs (Gorrono, 2023). AI-based language translation mechanisms will facilitate real-time translation in multiple languages and dialects. Speech-to-text and text-to-speech translation, combined with other technologies like VR (virtual reality) and AR (augmented reality), will make it easy for differently abled and special needs learners to pursue their education.

Another major benefit of employing AI is its ability to provide useful information related to learning issues among learners by examining student performance and other related data. By identifying patterns in learning difficulties, it will make educators aware of learners' needs at an early stage and support timely remedial.

Another positive facet of AI in education is that AI will holistically cater to helping educators (Gorrono, 2023), especially in the context of the large class size, diverse student population, and limited resources. AI will automate the daily tasks of lesson planning, timetable formation, grading, assessment, and progress tracking. The saved time can be used by educators to expand their pedagogical perspectives, engage in independent research, enhance their skills, and engage with students. AI will thus help to improve the quality of teachers and their teaching, encouraging learners to learn and improving the overall quality of education in the country.

Despite these advantages, there are many challenges that the Indian education system will have to encounter in harnessing AI (Melo, 2023). First, the impoverished technological infrastructure in rural India is a significant obstacle because AI requires electricity and internet connections, two major facilities that are not available in many parts of rural India. The cost of setting up AI-driven educational systems is high, and incurring the same would be difficult for both rural and urban educational institutions. In addition to this, incorporating AI would also include the additional cost of training educators and learners to use AI-driven mechanisms. Given the digital literacy divide in the country, training educators and learners would prove a costly and time-consuming affair. Moreover, there is still scepticism about ethical considerations, data privacy, and security when using AI. Robust measures will have to be taken to ensure the safe and secure use of data against misuse of personal data and algorithmic bias. In this context, administrators and policymakers will also have to devise and actualize strong regulations, ethical guidelines, and systems regarding the use of AI. Lastly, administrators and policymakers often express resistance to change and refrain from embracing change and innovation.

Conclusion

Achieving educational equality is a significant aspect of the National Education Policy 2020. Achieving educational equality in India is a challenging task because of various socio-economic, cultural, and geographical disparities in the country. In a situation where past policies have not completely succeeded in bringing about an inclusive and equal education system in India, AI comes across as a tool that will address the challenges. While harnessing AI promises equality in education by providing individualised education to learners, reducing educators' load and enhancing their skill set, and eliminating geographical barriers, it also poses challenges in terms of costs, training, digital literacy, privacy, and other ethical issues. The advantages certainly outweigh the challenges, as AI offers a wholesome solution to address a significant concern of educational equality for the country. Conducting pilot research and strategic planning for the phased implementation of AI in education will help make educational equality in India a reality. Overall, the present study contributes to the ongoing discussion on incorporating new technologies to stimulate progress in the Indian education system.

References

Arya, M.L. & Yadav, R. (2020). *A Critical Study of Indian Education System*. International Journal of Research and Analytical Reviews, 7(2). https://ijrar.org/papers/IJRAR2004134.pdf

Blanden, J., Doepke, M., & Stuhler, J. (2022). *Education Inequality*. Centre for Economic Performance. No. 1849. https://files.eric.ed.gov/fulltext/ED622182.pdf

Gorrono, N. (2023). *AI Unlocks Education's Future: Equal Access & Personalized Learning*. Savvity. https://www.savvity.com.au/blog/ai-unlocks-educations-future

Feng, W. (2023). *Advancing Educational Equality: Using AI Technology in K-12 English Language Education in Rural China*. The Asian

Conference on Education 2022. http://dx.doi.org/10.22492/issn.2186-5892.2023.68

Kumar, H. (2023). *Education in India: New Challenges and Issues.* International Journal of Creative Research Thoughts, 11(2). https://www.ijcrt.org/papers/IJCRT2302168.pdf

Kundu, P. (2014). *Major Dimensions of Inequalities in India: Education.* Centre for Budget and Governance Accountability. https://www.cbgaindia.org/wp-content/uploads/2016/04/Inequalities-in-Education.pdf

Melo, N. (2023). *Incorporating Artificial Intelligence into the Classroom: An Examination of Benefits, Challenges, and Best Practices.* eLearning Industry. https://elearningindustry.com/incorporating-artificial-intelligence-into-classroom-examination-benefits-challenges-and-best-practices

MHRD (2020). *National Education Policy 2020.* Government of India. https://www.education.gov.in/sites/upload_files/mhrd/files/NEP_Final_English_0.pdf

UNESCO (2023). *Artificial Intelligence in Education.* UNESCO. https://www.unesco.org/en/digital-education/artificial-intelligence

17. Integrating Technology to Inculcate Research Skills in Undergraduate Learners in India

Dr. Swati Bhise & Dr. Ramkishan Bhise

Introduction

Education is an indispensable tool for the advancement of individuals and society, and consequently it plays a vital role in crafting future generations. The transformative design of New Education Policy (NEP) of 2020 carries tremendous significance in India, a country where education is highly valued. It aims to provide a comprehensive and student-centered education system that prioritizes flexibility, skills, and knowledge that are relevant to the modern day.

A significant change in the way education is understood, planned, and provided has been brought by NEP 2020. It covers multiple factors, such as primary and secondary education, tertiary education as well as professional training, and the professional growth of educators. The 5+3+3+4 curricular frameworks are a fundamental component of the system, which replaces the previous 10+2 system. This new structure prioritizes the development of early childhood education, fundamental learning, and the cultivation of critical thinking abilities starting at a young age.

In today's fast-paced and global society, the ability to conduct research efficiently is an essential skill for undergraduate learners. Research skills not only enable students to effectively navigate the vast area of information, but also nurture critical thinking, problem-solving, and innovation. There is a noteworthy dearth in providing undergraduate learners with essential research skills in the Indian education. Conventional teaching methods frequently fail to offer students practical experience and opportunities to acquaint themselves with contemporary research tools and procedures.

The main focus of this research article is the integration of technology to improve research abilities among undergraduate learners in India, acknowledging the urgent need to bridge this gap. Indian educators have the ability to transform the learning process, enhancing its interactivity, engagement, and effectiveness in fostering skill acquisition by harnessing the capabilities of technology. This paper investigates several approaches, methodologies, and exemplary methods for incorporating technology into the undergraduate curriculum with the aim of nurturing a research-centered mindset among students.

By examining the present state and challenges of Indian Education, this research article aims to add to the ongoing discussion on educational reform in India. It offers important insights for educators, policymakers, and stakeholders involved in undergraduate education. The ultimate aim is to prepare competent researchers by providing th undergraduate learners with the necessary skills and information to excel in a highly competitive and ever-changing global environment. The research strives to offer insights into the following crucial domains:

1. The present state of research capabilities among undergraduate learners in India.

2. The impact of technology on the teaching-learning process and its ability to improve research abilities.

3. Case studies and illustrations of effective incorporation of technology in undergraduate education: domestic and global perspectives.

4. Practical ideas and instructions for educators and institutions to efficiently integrate technology into their teaching techniques.

The present state of research capabilities among undergraduate learners in India

The academic progress and career advancement of undergraduate students are significantly impacted by their research skills. But several challenges can be noticed in Indian higher education. The present state, challenges, and constraints pertaining to research skills among undergraduate students in India are analyzed in the following discussion. Further it offers insights into potential strategies to improve these capabilities. The challenges associated with research abilities among undergraduate students in India are discussed below.

Insufficient research exposure

The emphasis is placed on tests and grades rather than the development of research abilities in numerous undergraduate programmes. A stringent curriculum allows limited opportunities for interdisciplinary research or autonomous innovations. The prioritization of memorization-based learning and uniform evaluations dissuades learners from engaging in independent research endeavours beyond the established syllabus.

Scarcity of Resource

As a result of the restricted availability of research facilities, laboratories, and libraries undergraduate students in India encounter a significant problem in research skill development. The problems like limited funding for research programmes and limited infrastructure present additional challenges for students conducting investigations into research topics. Lick of resources obstruct students from doing comprehensive research and experimentation.

Expertise and Proficiency of Faculty

A very few faculty members actively include students in research, others may lack the necessary proficiency or motivation. The absence of consistent guidance has a detrimental effect on the quality of research carried out by undergraduate students. The involvement of faculty members plays a crucial role in cultivating research abilities in students, and the degree of their involvement significantly impacts students' research proficiency.

Curriculum Design

Assessments and grades are prioritized over the nurturing of research skills in many undergraduate programmes. A rigid curriculum restricts the chances for multidisciplinary research or independent exploration. The emphasis on rote learning and standardized assessments discourages students from pursuing independent inquiry beyond the prescribed curriculum.

Inadequate knowledge and motivation

In India a considerable amount of students is unaware of the benefits of research and lack the determination to engage in it. The employment possibilities and limited availability of research success stories act as an additional obstacle to participate in research. To develop a research-oriented environment among undergraduate students requires both raising awareness about the significance of research and providing motivations to stimulate student engagement.

Language Barriers

English as the main language for research poses challenges for non-English speaking learners. The extent to which students may access and contribute to scholarly literature is significantly impacted by their level of language competence. Overcoming language barriers is crucial for promoting inclusivity and diversity in research environments.

Evaluation criteria

The set of courses taught to undergraduate learners often do not adequately recognize or motivate research productivity. Lack of research motivation discourages students from actively engaging in research efforts. Students may be incentivized to actively participate in research efforts by applying rigorous evaluation methods that precisely scale the worth of research contributions.

The need for significant reforms in Indian educational institutions is highlighted by the challenges associated with research abilities among undergraduate students. To foster a group of skilled researchers and innovators, it is imperative to address a range of obstacles, including insufficient exposure to research culture, resource constraints, lack of expertise in faculty, inadequacies in curriculum development, a lack of awareness and motivation, language barriers, and ineffective assessment techniques. India has the potential to utilize the skills and capabilities of its undergraduate to make substantial advancements in several industries by establishing a conducive research atmosphere.

The impact of technology on the pedagogy and its ability to improve research abilities

Over the past few decades, technology has completely transformed education and research, leading to substantial changes in how we teach, learn, and conduct research. Let's explore the ways in which technology has influenced various domains.

Optimized Educational Experience

Technology has optimized educational experience by online learning opportunities, global access to education and adaptive learning. Technology provides interactive and captivating learning opportunities through the use of multimedia tools, simulations, and virtual laboratories like MOOCs and EdTech, Coursera and edX. These technologies support the learners for the dynamic exploration of intricate concepts, thereby expanding their comprehension and retention of information. Geographical limitations are eliminated by online courses and digital materials. It has allowed learners to obtain high-quality education from any location with internet access, promoting inclusivity and diversity in education.

Personalized learning or adaptive learning platforms utilize algorithms to customize content based on individual student requirements, facilitating independent learning and successfully addressing areas of weakness. Hence, the supportiveness of technology in the research will be beneficial.

Research Skills

The use of technology in research has growing since last two decades. There are many tools available to aid in research process like direct access to the information, data collection, and collaboration and last but not the least citation generation.

Digital libraries, online journals, and databases like Google books project Gutenberg, JSTOR, Google Scholar and others provide immediate access to a vast amount of scholarly information, enabling researchers to stay informed about the most recent research advancements and study a wide range of perspectives.

Technology offers effective tools like the SPSS software that supports in analyzing statistical data, Excel, Tableau or Python for gathering data, conducting surveys, and doing experiments, allowing researchers to acquire and analyze extensive datasets, detect patterns, and derive significant conclusions with efficiency.

Virtual collaboration tools enable academics to interact internationally, exchanging research findings, working together on projects, and participating in live conversations, so promoting the development of a global research community.

Tools such as EndNote, BibMe, Automated Citation Machines, and Zotero facilitate the process of referring and citing sources, making the research process more efficient and guaranteeing precision and uniformity in citations.

Models of Blended Learning

There are different models blended learning. Like Hybrid approach, Synchronous and asynchronous learning methods. The hybrid approach combines in-person teaching with online elements to enhance learning experiences, providing flexibility and personalized learning opportunities. Flipped classrooms, which involve students interacting with educational material prior to class, are becoming increasingly popular due to their ability to enhance student engagement and involvement.

Technology enables both synchronous and asynchronous learning methods. Synchronous learning involves real-time contacts, such as through webinars and video conferencing. Asynchronous learning, on the other hand, allows for self-paced learning through recorded lectures and discussion forums. These options accommodate various learning preferences and schedules.

Ethics and integrity in research

Technology assists in the identification of plagiarized content, thereby ensuring academic integrity and upholding ethical standards in research.

Researchers must address ethical dilemmas pertaining to data privacy, informed consent, and digital rights, assuring ethical behaviour throughout the research process and upholding participants' rights and anonymity.

To summarize, although technology provides a significant opportunity to improve education and research capacities, it is crucial to handle the related problems and considerations in order to fully exploit its potential benefits and promote a flourishing digital learning and research environment.

Case studies and illustrations of effective incorporation of technology in undergraduate education, derived from both domestic and global perspectives

Various cases studies and illustrations of successful technology integration in undergraduate education offers useful insights into the actual implementation of technology in teaching and learning approaches. Below are three cases that exemplify successful deployments, both within a country and on an international scale

Case Study 1: Integration of Information and Communication Technology (ICT) in Malaysian Schools

The integration of Information, Communication, and Technology (ICT) have been strategically prioritized in Malaysian schools. The significance of using technology for the purposes of teaching and learning is acknowledged by the Malaysian Ministry of Education.

In Kuala Lumpur, Simin Ghavifekr and Wan Athirah Wan Rosdy conducted research to look into the effects of integrating ICT in classrooms. The research revealed that thee teachers who are well-equipped and proficient in using ICT technologies can significantly improve the quality of teaching and enhance student learning results. Furthermore, teacher professional development programmes play a crucial role in enhancing their competence in incorporating technology into classroom teaching.

The need of equipping teachers with sufficient training and tools to properly utilize technology is highlighted by this case study. This case study showcases the significant impact that focused professional development programmes may have on teaching methods and student achievements.

Case Study 2: Research and development in the field of STEM education

There is an increasing focus on Science, Technology, Engineering, and Mathematics (STEM) education in the horizons of international education. The technology plays vital role in improving STEM learning experiences and cultivating students' enthusiasm and expertise in these disciplines.

Continuous research and development endeavours in STEM education emphasize the revolutionary influence of technology although not exclusive to India. This Research has examined many strategies for incorporating digital tools, simulations, and interactive platforms into STEM classrooms in order to encourage active learning and foster critical thinking.

This case study highlights the significance of utilizing technology to improve STEM education. The statement underscores the importance of employing inventive pedagogical approaches and technological tools to actively involve students in STEM fields.

Case Study 3: The Revolutionary Influence of Technology in Indian Higher Education

In India, educational institutions are progressively embracing technology-based methods for teaching and learning. This transition is clearly demonstrated by the extensive implementation of Learning Management Systems (LMS), virtual laboratories, online examinations, and other digital tools.

Indian educational institutions like IIMT University, Meerut, Amity University, NMIMS University and others are utilizing technology to establish interactive and tailored learning environments. These efforts seek to improve student involvement, enable cooperative learning, and offer access to a wide variety of educational materials. This case study exemplifies the profound influence of technology on higher education in

India. This emphasizes the significance of digital tools and platforms in enhancing teaching and learning experiences, therefore empowering both students and educators.

These case studies demonstrate how technology integration is improving undergraduate education on a domestic and worldwide scale. Through the acquisition of knowledge from successful implementations and the utilization of optimal methods, educators can proficiently utilize technology to establish captivating, all-encompassing, and efficient learning environments for students.

Strategies to Improve Research Skills Among Undergraduate Students in India

There are various possibilities for enhancing the research skills and to tackle the difficulties the undergraduate students encounter during research. This section scrutinizes possible strategies and efforts that educational institutions, faculty members, and policymakers might adopt to create a favourable atmosphere for research among undergraduate students.

Curriculum Reforms

Incorporating research-oriented courses, workshops, and seminars into undergraduate programmes can provide students with crucial research skills and experience. These courses encompass subjects such as research procedures, literature review techniques, data analysis, and academic writing. Moreover, fostering interdisciplinary research and project-based learning enables students to delve into several disciplines and apply their knowledge in practical situations. Institutions can enhance students' preparedness for research endeavours by integrating research-focused components into the curriculum.

Faculty Development Programs

Investing in faculty development programmes is essential for developing mentorship skills and cultivating a research-oriented mentality among educators. Training workshops can equip faculty members with techniques for proficiently assisting students in navigating the research process, providing valuable feedback, and fostering self-directed investigation. Institutions can make a substantial contribution to the development of research capacities among undergraduates by enabling faculty members to effectively mentor students. Institutions should prioritize offering thorough training programs for educators to proficiently use technology in their teaching methods. Providing workshops, webinars, and continuous support can assist teachers in smoothly incorporating digital tools into their classes, resulting in optimal benefits for both educators and students.

Personalized learning using digital tools

By using digital tools that cater to unique learning styles and paces educators can allow students to take control of their learning journey. GoGuardian and similar tools provide customized resources and support for students to review coursework independently, access supplementary materials, and explore more challenging subjects.

Virtual Connections Beyond the Classroom

Technology enables students to interact with classmates from different backgrounds and professionals in different professions, fostering global ties. Engaging in virtual conversations and interviews with students from different countries promotes cultural exchange and expands viewpoints. Social media platforms allow students to engage with professionals, experts, and government officials, enhancing classroom discussions with practical knowledge. Virtual reality (VR) technology can transfer students to distant destinations like monuments, museums, or historical sites, improving their learning and appreciation of various cultures and contexts.

Online Courses and E-Learning

Enhancing traditional classroom teaching with online courses and e-learning platforms provides students with chances for self-directed learning and skill enhancement. Coursera and similar platforms offer a wide range of courses covering various areas and fields, enabling students to delve into topics outside their regular curriculum.

Research Cells and Clubs

The creation of student-led research cells inside institutions fosters chances for peer collaboration and mentorship. These cells have the ability to coordinate a range of events, including conferences, symposia, and research competitions, with the purpose of presenting student research projects and promoting a culture of inquiry. Institutions can foster research enthusiasm and offer opportunities for students to showcase their work by actively engaging them in the planning and implementation of research-related activities.

Digital Literacy

Enhancing students' digital literacy involves the imperative task of promoting digital research tools and databases, which are crucial for enabling them to effectively traverse the digital research environment. Educational institutions can provide instructional sessions or workshops focused on utilizing internet databases, citation management software, and research collaboration platforms. In addition, improving students' capacity to critically assess internet material guarantees their ability to differentiate reliable sources and steer clear of misinformation, thus raising the quality of their research findings.

Collaborations, partnerships, and communication tools

Collaborations and partnerships are important for connecting students with industry partners, research organizations, and other universities. This allows students to gain practical research experience and broaden their professional network. Institutions can form alliances with organizations that share students' research interests, creating avenues for internships, collaborative research initiatives, and guidance from experts in the business. Collaborative programmes boost students' research experiences and improve their employability skills by connecting academics and industry. Tools like Google Workspace and Microsoft Teams enable smooth communication and cooperation between students and educators. These systems facilitate collaboration among students on projects, resource sharing, and real-time feedback, creating a dynamic and engaging learning setting.

Assessment and Feedback

Digital assessment technologies facilitate the grading process and allow educators to offer prompt and helpful feedback to students. Turnitin and similar platforms identify plagiarism and support academic integrity by fostering originality and correct citation methods.

Flipped Classroom Approach

The flipped classroom model reverses the conventional teaching method by providing educational material outside of class hours, enabling more interactive and stimulating in-class exercises. Assigning pre-recorded lectures or reading materials as homework allows for more class time to be dedicated to debates, problem-solving, and hands-on activities, which can improve student engagement and comprehension.

Accessibility and Inclusivity

Making sure that technology is available to all students, including those with impairments is crucial. To engage every student completely and to derive value from the educational process it is important to offer many formats for content, such as video captions and text-to-speech software.

Data-Driven Decision Making

Utilizing data analytics technologies enables instructors to monitor student advancement, pinpoint areas for enhancement, and customize instructional methods to successfully address individual requirements. Educators can enhance learning outcomes and support student success by examining student data to make well-informed decisions.

Stay alert and adaptive

It is crucial for educators and institutions to keep up to date with the most recent tools and trends in educational technology due to the swift rate of technological progress. Receiving feedback from students and adjusting teaching methods accordingly helps instructors provide top-notch instruction that matches the changing demands of learners in the digital era.

Educational institutions, professors, and policymakers can contribute to the development of strong research aptitude by incorporating these possibilities for enhancement among undergraduate students in India. For nurturing future researchers and innovators Institutions may foster an optimal environment by implementing curriculum changes, providing faculty development opportunities, encouraging student-led research endeavours, promoting digital literacy, and establishing collaborative relationships. It is essential to invest in these techniques in order to cultivate a culture of research and innovation that enables undergraduate students to tackle intricate difficulties and make significant progress in their respective areas of study.

Conclusion

The objective of this paper is to integrate technology and provide a transformational technique to improve research abilities among undergraduate students to promote research skills in India closely coincides with the objectives of the National Education Policy (NEP) of 2020. An educational environment that is learner-centric and technologically driven, emphasizing personalized learning experiences, critical thinking, and creativity is promoted by the NEP. Technology allows students to build autonomy by engaging with personalized learning opportunities further, it allows them to explore topics at their own pace and interact with customized content that enhances their research abilities. Adaptive assessment methods enhance these skills by offering instant feedback and directing learners towards effective research methods. Data-driven decision-making enables instructors to pinpoint areas needing improvement and customize educational approaches to ensure optimal skill enhancement. The NEP's dedication to accessibility and inclusivity highlights the significance of technology in ensuring equal access to research materials and opportunities for individuals from various linguistic and geographical backgrounds. Educational technology, known as EdTech, is crucial in providing platforms and tools that allow direct interaction with learners and enable access to virtual labs, online libraries, and collaborative forums.

Integrating technology promotes the National Education Policy's objectives and enables learners to actively contribute to the progress of knowledge and societal development, preparing them for success in the digital era.

References

Abdolrezapour, P., Ganjeh, S. J., & Ghanbari, N. (2023, May 23). *Self-efficacy and resilience as predictors of students' academic motivation in online education*. PLOS ONE. ttps://doi.org/10.1371/journal.pone.0285984

Carstens, Mallon, Bataineh, & Al-Bataineh. (2021, January). *Effects of Technology on Student Learning*. TOJET: The Turkish Online Journal of Educational Technology, 20(1). https://files.eric.ed.gov/fulltext/EJ1290791.pdf

Council, F. T. (2019, January 29). *14 Practical Ways to Integrate Technology into The Classroom*. Forbes. https://www.forbes.com/sites/forbestechcouncil/2019/01/29/14-practical-ways-to-integrate-technology-into-the-classroom/?sh=68cdfb5c7e77

Doğan, B., & Robin, B. (2015, January 1). *Technology's Role in Stem Education and the Stem SOS Model*. SensePublishers eBooks. https://doi.org/10.1007/978-94-6300-019-2_6

Ghavifekr, & Wan Rosdy. (2015). *Teaching and Learning with Technology: Effectiveness of ICT Integration in Schools*. International Journal of Research in Education and Science, 1(2), 175–191. https://files.eric.ed.gov/fulltext/EJ1105224.pdf

Gilbertson, N. (2007, November 6). *How to Integrate Technology*. Edutopia. https://www.edutopia.org/technology-integration-guide-implementation

Heick, T. (2023, March 13). *How Technology Changed Teaching and Learning*. TeachThought. https://www.teachthought.com/the-future-of-learning/how-technology-changed-teaching/

Joubert, S. (2023, August 31). *How Teachers Are Integrating Technology into the Classroom*. Graduate Blog.

https://graduate.northeastern.edu/resources/integrating-technology-into-teaching/

Kaminskienė, L., Järvelä, S., & Lehtinen, E. (2022, December 27). *How does technology challenge teacher education?* International Journal of Educational Technology in Higher Education. https://doi.org/10.1186/s41239-022-00375-1

Kumari, & Nigam. (2023). *Technology Integration in Education: A Catalyst for Transforming Learning—The New Education Policy 2020 Perspective.* International Journal of Creative Research Thoughts (IJCRT) International Open Access, Peer-Reviewed, Refereed Journal, 11 (Issue 9), 11 (Issue 9). https://ijcrt.org/papers/IJCRT2309306.pdf

Kumari. (2022, February 6). *The Impact of Technology on Classroom Learning.* IIMT University Official Blog. Retrieved February 22, 2024, from https://iimtu.edu.in/blog/the-impact-of-technology-on-classroom-learning/

Li, Y., & Wang, T. (2011, January 1). *The Cultivation of Research Capability for Undergraduate.* Communications in Computer and Information Science. https://doi.org/10.1007/978-3-642-24022-5_72

Li, Y., Wang, K., Xiao, Y., & Froyd, J. E. (2020, March 10). *Research and trends in STEM education: a systematic review of journal publications.* International Journal of STEM Education. https://doi.org/10.1186/s40594-020-00207-6

Mardiana. (2020, June). *Lecturers' Adaptability to Technological Change and Its Impact On the Teaching Process.* Jurnal Pendidikan Indonesia (JPI), 9(2), 275–289. https://doi.org/10.23887/jpi-undiksha.v9i2.24595

Mugabo, E., Velin, L., & Nduwayezu, R. (2021, April 26). *Exploring factors associated with research involvement of undergraduate students at the College of Medicine and Health Sciences, University of Rwanda.* BMC Medical Education. https://doi.org/10.1186/s12909-021-02662-3

Reyaz Ahmad Bhat. (2023, August 17). *The Impact of Technology Integration on Student Learning Outcomes: A Comparative Study.* International Journal of Social Science, Educational, Economics, Agriculture Research and Technology (IJSET), 2(9), 592–596. https://doi.org/10.54443/ijset.v2i9.218

Timotheou, S., Miliou, O., Dimitriadis, Y., Sobrino, S. V., Giannoutsou, N., Cachia, R., Martínez-Monés, A., & Ioannou, A. (2022, November 21). *Impacts of digital technologies on education and factors influencing schools' digital capacity and transformation: A literature review.* Education and Information Technologies. https://doi.org/10.1007/s10639-022-11431-8

Topp, Mortenson, & Grandgenett. (2006, November 13). Six Objectives for Technology Infusion into Teacher Education: a model in action. Journal of Information Technology for Teacher Education, 57–69. https://doi.org/10.1080/0962029960050107

Triplett, W. J. (2023, September 11). *Impact of Technology Integration in STEM Education.* Cybersecurity and Innovative Technology Journal. https://doi.org/10.53889/citj.v1i1.295

Vahidy, J. (2019, July 12). *Enhancing STEM Learning Through Technology.* Pressbooks. https://pressbooks.pub/techandcurr2019/chapter/enhancingstem/

18. Recent Advance in Educational Pedagogies

Dr. Parag Bhalchandra, Dr. Vaijayanta Patil, Dr. Mahesh Joshi & Dr. Ashok Gingine

Introduction

The term 'pedagogy' is derived from the ancient Greek word pedagogies, which means a slave who led children to school. This is why it is inadequate for post-school years when students are usually independent and self-guided [1]. The conventional view of pedagogy as the "science or art of teaching" conflicts with their desired focus on the process of learning [1]. The field of pedagogy is centred around the instant perception of the teaching scenario. Pedagogy is the art of developing strategies via hands-on experience in unique and practical contexts [2]. Any theory of pedagogy worth defending in the field of education must demonstrate the complementary nature of situational practice and explicit teaching [3]. The use of pedagogical educational technology (PET) has transformed the way students learn and teachers interact in contemporary educational systems [4]. The goal of recent advances in educational pedagogies is to improve teaching and learning by integrating technology into existing methods. This would benefit both students and teachers. In the world of education, there are two main models: traditional classroom instruction and more modern hybrid approaches. Most classrooms still use the time-honored synchronous approach, in which teachers and students engage in real-time, spatially bound interactions. Synchronous learning describes a synchronous approach to education. The dissemination of knowledge within a learning community through interactions involving both in-person and online learning methods. This approach to education combines both conventional classroom instruction and more modern, asynchronous forms of online learning [5].

Using technology in the classroom, students are exposed to a variety of stimuli, allowing for more active learning. With the use of technology, subjects become more engaging. Media literacy is enhanced for both students and teachers [7]. The networked educator, seen in Fig. 1, makes use of several technological devices.

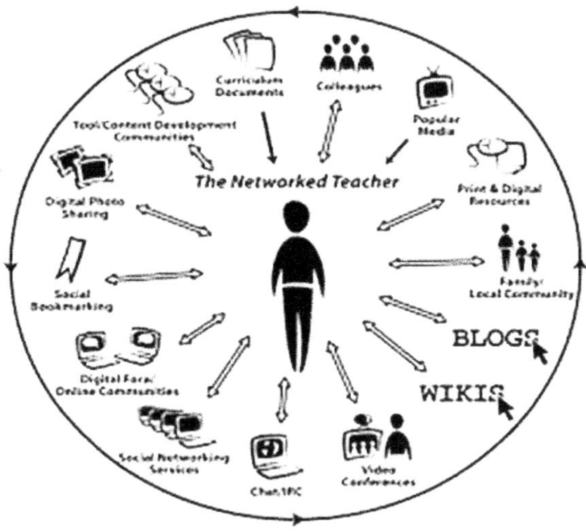

Fig.1 Utilization of technology and gadgets [7].

Methods of instruction, collaboration in the workplace, and course development were all impacted by innovation pedagogy as an educational strategy [8]. The next section would discuss innovation pedagogy.

Innovative Pedagogies

Good teaching methods have the potential to have a beneficial effect on pupils. The focus of educational pedagogy in recent years has shifted from the instructor to the student. Consequently, numerous classical research has employed diverse pedagogical approaches to establish an efficient educational system. Consequently, this study aims to examine how students respond to several modern pedagogical strategies [9]. Scholars from the global South are suggesting that colleges must be decolonized as enter in a new era of education where virtual learning and teaching modalities are likely to gain popularity [10], raising concerns about the shift towards the virtual when many communities face challenges in accessing the internet and the necessary technology to participate [11].

Literature reviews

Recent Advances in Educational pedagogy hold great importance in teaching. The review found that some prior relevant studies were examined by researchers and authors.

Muniandy et al., (2023) [12] investigated the effects of several contemporary instructional approaches on students. Educational data from a worldwide perspective was also an aim, as was an evaluation of various educational stances. Pedagogical approaches from a Malaysian viewpoint were also examined in the study. Finally, the article covered the latest advancements that would be used in the future to improve schooling. There was an exploration of many learning and teaching styles, so teachers may pick the one that works best for them and then use it with their pupils according to their abilities. Future pedagogical innovations were also detailed, providing researchers with a road map on where to direct their attention for maximum impact.

Obidovna et al., (2023) [13] delved into the significant issue of adjusting teaching methods to match contemporary educational trends considering the pedagogical element. Teachers were required to continuously enhance and modify their teaching methods in response to the evolving technological landscape and the evolving educational requirements of their students. Important pedagogical elements of teaching methods were covered in the paper, along with strategies for improving the quality of education. The study offered advice to educators who wish to effectively incorporate innovations into their pedagogical practices and examines real-world instances of modifying instructional approaches.

Zembylas et al., (2022) [14] proposed a theory based on the idea of emotive atmospheres to explain the spread of democracy and democratic teaching in educational settings. This study aimed to determine the conditions under which emotional environments might be felt or even "created," including the emotional and material aspects that undermine democracy, democratic education, and right-wing populism. The author sought to make the atmosphere more approachable by following a line of thinking that acknowledges the emotive power of democracy and right-wing populism. The author then posed the question of how democratic education may react by paying close attention to democracy as something that is effectively delivered and created. In light of the growing influence of right-wing populist ideologies, the study also tried to identify ways to revitalize the emotional climates of democratic teaching within educational institutions. This analysis added to the growing body of work regarding the difficulty of resisting right-wing populist affectivity through democratic education.

Reis, Sally M et al., (2021) [15] developed enrichment pedagogy in part by the gifted education field and listed various forms of this engaging instructional strategy, such as interest-based learning pedagogy, curriculum compacting and differentiation, project-based learning, open-ended choice, and the application of creative productivity to students' learning. This specialized pedagogy was highlighted by the author, who also provided instances of how enrichment experts and school counselors might apply these engaging tactics in the classroom, with students who were academically gifted and with typically developing academic skills. This study wraps up with a concise review of studies that show the favorable effects of this kind of instruction on pupils over time.

Motala et al., (2021) [16] examined three specific areas of the decolonized curriculum and teaching methods from the perspective of the students. First, the author looked at the sociality that was encouraged in education. Given that one of education's primary purposes was to help students and teachers become more integrated members of society, it's natural to wonder how students and teachers could interact in a decolonized classroom, especially considering the recent COVID-19 scandal. Secondly, the study looked at participation patterns, which included academic activities and the assistance that was given. Third, while taking linguistic concerns into account, the author examined the knowledge forms and canons to which students were exposed in their programs. Finally, this study delved into the curriculum's decolonization within the framework of the COVID-19 pandemic.

Abdunabievich et al., (2022) [17] categorized several pedagogical technologies according to the following: preschool, elementary, basic, extracurricular-additional, secondary special, vocational, and higher education (based on the kinds of continuing education, retraining, and advanced training). At the same time, Languages spoken at home and abroad, literature, social and precise sciences, arts, sports, engineering, technology, applied sciences, occupations, and specialized educational pedagogical tools are all part of the educational landscape.

Dreamson et al., (2020) [18] divided this study into four sections. First one was argued that studio-based learning has developed a 'resistant' stance towards online education, which justifies the omission of understanding connective features from its discourses. Second, this critical analysis compares four recent studies on online design education, analyzing each from a technical and pedagogical perspective. Third, the purpose of introducing meta-connective pedagogy is to discuss the reasons and mechanisms behind the rise of connectivity as a pedagogical issue in online education. Fourth and last, the formulation of a conceptual form of meta-connective design education is discussed, along with the new duties and contributions of educators. All things considered; the notion of design education was supposedly turned upside down in favour of more efficient connectivity that included the social aspects of conventional design studios.

Strobl et al., (2020) [19] provided a study of technologies that support writing instruction in secondary and higher education focusing on instructional affordances based on technological specifications. The review addressed tools that help writers who were first or second language learners. The author laid out a comprehensive review of 44 tools covering 26 quantitative and qualitative aspects of writing processes, instructional methods, feedback forms, and technical requirements. When it came to the educational emphasis, there were a lot of tools that helped with micro-level revisions (such as grammar, spelling, and word frequencies) that targeted factual knowledge, but there were not many tools that helped with macro-level revisions (such as argumentative structure and rhetorical moves) that encouraged self-monitoring and the development of writing strategies.

Brownel et al., (2019) [20] outlined a framework to help teacher candidates understand how to apply high-leverage practices (HLPs) and described pedagogies that might be applied in teacher training in a variety of contexts, from college classrooms to P-12 settings. Starting with analyzing videos, doing case studies, practicing, and using virtual simulations, these "pedagogies of enactment" should progress to more realistic contexts where teaching practices can be put into practice, culminating in classroom settings where coaching is available, methods include coordinated field excursions, planned tutoring, and lesson study. In this study, research in cognitive science and professional expertise development was utilized by the author to identify effective pedagogies in the field of teacher education. These pedagogies could be utilized to support candidates' learning as they progress through the program.

Mynbayeva et al., (2018) [21] provided a concise overview of the recent developments in didactics on the implementation of new approaches to education and the investigation of educators' comprehension of these shifts. The author of this study took four factors into account: the growth of pedagogy as a field, an ecological perspective on education, the impact of the digital age on classroom practices, and new approaches to instruction. Literally and metaphorically, there were two tiers to the philosophy of education. Education is becoming more decentralized and diverse, with an emphasis on globalization, and digital technologies are being integrated at a macro level within the "education-society" link. Combining an activity approach with an energy-informational environment approach, cognition with constructivism and connectivism, and an active mix of classic and novel approaches were all present at the micro-level in the "teacher-learner" connection.

Seatter et al., (2017) [22] redefined, clarified, and provided a more systematic and holistic understanding of a transformational pedagogy essential for learning, this paper used an epistemological and pedagogical analysis of pertinent literature. In the main argument, three pedagogical models and three sustainability curriculum positions were compared. These models differ significantly in how they prioritize the learner's prior knowledge and beliefs, how they engage the learner, and the possibility of critical thinking and transformative learning. To help civilizations become more sustainable, it has been discovered that a transformative pedagogy might overcome and eliminate paradoxes.

Askerc Veniger et al., (2016) [23] found that instructors' views on first and sustained PTCs differed significantly. It is commonly believed that higher education institutions should hire people with experience teaching in elementary or secondary schools. Those in higher-ranking positions gave sustained PTCs the least weight. Compared to respondents who did not take part in PTCs, those who did participate in (short) PTCs placed less value on PT and the certificate of participation in PT. On the other hand, those who had the most PT experience (51 hours or more) was more likely to support PTCs, lending credence to the hypothesis that longer courses had a greater impact on educators' pedagogical stances and ideas about education than shorter ones.

Guðjónsdóttir., (2016) [24] highlighted diversity and inclusion in this study as a process that never ends. Social justice, democracy, human rights, and universal education were its guiding principles. Three terms were used to describe inclusion: (i) the term "inclusive education," which refers to the steps taken to broaden participation and narrow exclusion; (ii) a method of instruction that prioritizes the needs of all students; and (iii) The term "inclusive practice" refers to the actual ways in which the idea of inclusion is put into action. Besides, as educators plan lessons, lead classroom discussions, and work together, this study outlined essential strategies for cultivating inclusive practice. Creating fair opportunities for all students to succeed in science is necessary since science education is vital for all people.

Korthagen et al., (2016) [25] described pedagogical techniques that were necessary for teaching about teaching, which differ significantly from the approaches that govern instruction in schools. This study started with Several traditions that have developed out of the 50-year-old divide between competency-based and teacher-centred systems. The results of these traditions' empirical studies were reviewed. Next, an overview was presented of several specific pedagogical strategies and techniques, and the research on these topics was discussed. Lastly, research-based principles for effective pedagogies of teacher education were developed after discussing underlying tensions in the field and viable options for resolving these issues.

Hegarty et al., (2015) [26] proposed a model, Open Educational Resources (OER) along with the flood of digital information, which revolutionized education. After defining open pedagogy and providing some background on the topic, the author used recent studies to outline eight characteristics of this approach to education that are based on Open Educational Practice (OEP) and the idea of transparency. Educators have numerous obstacles when it comes to participatory technologies since they might not understand how to effectively utilize them to influence the changing dynamic of the learning culture.

Conclusion and Future Scope

Advanced educational pedagogies enhance the effectiveness of the teaching and learning process. This review emphasizes the dynamic character of educational practices, the significance of adjusting to technological advances, and the beneficial effects of a supportive pedagogical environment on educators and students. The teaching methods and relevant technologies are being changed according to their demands and requirements. The various key themes and major points of previous and recent pedagogies have been discussed in this study. These factors highlight the well-strategy of educational pedagogy recently with standardized techniques. Offering a thorough review of the challenges, innovations, and considerations in modern teaching and learning contexts, these studies provided significant insights into several areas of pedagogy and education. Future research could benefit from a more focused effort to determine the long-term impacts of innovative instructional techniques on learners and educators alike.

References

Abdunabievich, Fazliddin Abdurazaqov, Fazliddin Odinaboboev Baxriddin Ugli, and Nozimakhon Donaeva Norbutaevna. "*Types of Pedagogical Technologies That Correspond to the Specifics of Moral and Aesthetic Education and Teaching of Students*." European Scholar Journal 3, no. 3 (2022): 68-74.

Askerc Veniger, Katarina. "*University teachers' opinions about higher education pedagogical training courses in Slovenia*." CEPS journal 6, no. 4 (2016): 141-161.

Beetham, Helen, and Rhona Sharpe. "*An introduction to rethinking pedagogy*." In Rethinking pedagogy for a digital age, pp. 1-14. Routledge, 2019.

Brownell, Mary T., Amber E. Benedict, Melinda M. Leko, David Peyton, Daisy Pua, and Catherine Richards-Tutor. "*A continuum of pedagogies for preparing teachers to use high-leverage practices."* Remedial and Special Education 40, no. 6 (2019): 338-355.

Dei, G. *Decolonizing the university: The challenges and possibilities of inclusive education.* Soc. Stud. Études Soc. 2016, 11, 23.

Diamond, Zane M. *"Old pedagogies for wise education: A janussian reflection on universities."* Philosophies 6, no. 3 (2021): 64.

Djalilova, Zarnigor. *"PEDAGOGICAL EDUCATIONAL TECHNOLOGY: ESSENCE, CHARACTERISTICS AND EFFICIENCY."* Академические исследования в современной науке 2, no. 23 (2023): 29-38.

Dreamson, Neal. *"Online design education: meta-connective pedagogy."* International Journal of Art & Design Education 39, no. 3 (2020): 483-497.

Fawns, Tim. *"An entangled pedagogy: Looking beyond the pedagogy— technology dichotomy."* Postdigital Science and Education 4, no. 3 (2022): 711-728.

Guðjónsdóttir, Hafdís, and Edda Óskarsdóttir. *"Inclusive education, pedagogy and practice."* Science education towards inclusion (2016): 7-22.

Hegarty, Bronwyn. *"Attributes of open pedagogy: A model for using open educational resources."* Educational technology (2015)

Khairnar, C. M. *"Advance pedagogy: Innovative methods of teaching and learning."* International journal of information and education technology 5, no. 11 (2015): 869.

Konst, Taru, and Liisa Kairisto-Mertanen. *"Developing innovation pedagogy approach."* On the Horizon 28, no. 1 (2020): 45-54.

Korthagen, Fred AJ. *"Pedagogy of teacher education."* International Handbook of Teacher Education: Volume 1 (2016): 311-346.

Macleod, Flora, and Michael Golby. *"Theories of Learning and Pedagogy: issues for teacher development."* Teacher Development 7, no. 3 (2003): 345-361.

Motala, Shireen, Yusuf Sayed, and Tarryn de Kock. *"Epistemic decolonization in reconstituting higher education pedagogy in South Africa: the student perspective."* Teaching in Higher Education 26, no. 7-8 (2021): 1002-1018.

Muniandy, Thayalan, and Norazilawati Abdullah. *"A Comprehensive Review: An Innovative Pedagogy for Future Education."* International

Journal of Online Pedagogy and Course Design (IJOPCD) 13, no. 1 (2023): 1-15.

Muniandy, Thayalan, and Norazilawati Abdullah. "*A Comprehensive Review: An Innovative Pedagogy for Future Education*." International Journal of Online Pedagogy and Course Design (IJOPCD) 13, no. 1 (2023): 1-15.

Murphy, Patricia. "*Defining pedagogy*." In Equity in the classroom, pp. 17-30. Routledge, 2003.

Mynbayeva, Aigerim, Zukhra Sadvakassova, and Bakhytkul Akshalova. "*Pedagogy of the twenty-first century: Innovative teaching methods*." New Pedagogical Challenges in the 21st Century. Contributions of Research in Education 7 (2018): 564-578.

Obidovna, Djalilova Zarnigor. "*ADAPTING TEACHING METHODS TO MODERN EDUCATIONAL TRENDS: PEDAGOGICAL ASPECT*." International Journal of Pedagogics 3, no. 10 (2023): 72-77.

Reis, Sally M., Sara Jane Renzulli, and Joseph S. Renzulli. "*Enrichment and gifted education pedagogy to develop talents, gifts, and creative productivity*." Education Sciences 11, no. 10 (2021): 615.

Seatter, Carol Scarff, and Kim Ceulemans. "*Teaching Sustainability in Higher Education: Pedagogical Styles that Make a Difference*." Canadian Journal of Higher Education 47, no. 2 (2017): 47-70.

Strobl, Carola, Emilie Ailhaud, Kalliopi Benetos, Ann Devitt, Otto Kruse, Antje Proske, and Christian Rapp. "*Digital support for academic writing: A review of technologies and pedagogies*." Computers & education 131 (2019): 33-48.

W. Nancy et al. / Procedia Computer Science 172 (2020) 382–388

Zembylas, Michalinos. "*The affective atmospheres of democratic education: pedagogical and political implications for challenging right-wing populism*." Discourse: Studies in the Cultural Politics of Education 43, no. 4 (2022): 556-570.

19. Multilingualism and NEP 2020

Dr. Manisha Kale & Dr. Dipak Wayal

India has always been a multiracial, multiethnic and multilingual country. Indian multilingualism is unique and also dynamic in nature. Online Webster's Dictionary defines multilingualism as "…using or able to use several languages especially with equal fluency". Wikipedia identifies multilingualism as "…the use of two or more languages, either by an individual speaker or by a community of speakers" and it also says that "…multilingual speakers outnumber monolingual speakers in the world's population". Accepting multilingualism in constitution and reorganization of the geographical boundaries within the nation as linguistic states was a major step in the management of multilingualism. Multilingualism is considered as the rule today and mono-lingualism is exception. Indian multilingualism is unique and also dynamic in nature; none of these terms captures the real texture of Indian multilingualism and it has no parallel anywhere in the world. In India language is written in many scripts and many languages are written in one script. Though they belong to different linguistic families they share many linguistic features. In India, six decades ago multiplicity of languages was considered as a problem to be solved or resolved and now due to its language management initiatives, multiplicity of languages is considered as a resource to be properly utilized. Language in India is closely tied to the culture. It offers a smorgasbord of numerous languages which makes this land the most vibrant language laboratory of the world. Chomsky claims that we can talk about 'languages' at least at two levels. At one level we have 'externalized language' that we hear and see and recognize as Hindi, Bengali, etc. at the other, we have 'internalized language' that underlies all visible/audible 'externalized language'. We know little about latter, because, as Chomsky claims, we know 'so little … about relevant aspects of the brain that we can hardly even speculate about what the connections might be…' (Chomsky 1986: 39).

The 2001 Census reported that there are a total of 122 languages and 234 mother tongues (Census India, 2010-11). 'The Constitution of India was framed with the provision that the official language of the Union

"

would be Hindi in Devnagari script with international numerals' (Das Gupta, 1970: 136). The Minister of State for Home said that "…Centre was committed to giving due recognition to all the languages through a proper mechanism of evaluation. The most important part is to differentiate between a language and a dialect. There should be proper guidelines to determine a language's status…" [The Hindu: Aug 11, 2009] The Official Languages Act, 1963 enacted to 'provide for the languages which may be used for the official purposes of the Union, for transacting the business in Parliament, for Central and State Acts and …' makes provision for the continuation of the use of English in addition to Hindi for all the official purposes of the Union for which it was being used immediately before that day, and for the transaction of business in Parliament, use of English for communication between the Union and a State which has not adopted Hindi as its official language, communication in Hindi to be accompanied by its English translation if the receiving State of the concerned communication has not adopted Hindi as the official language. The speakers of different languages speak more than one language reflecting the social, geographical and political realities. The language laws are codified to regulate the use of such diversity of languages. Language law empowers a language and its speakers. It is the regulation that controls the use of language(s) in general and specific domains in the society. The systematic coding of the written law is the contribution of British in India. It was intended for the convenience of the western model of governance. There is certainly some significant growth in multilingual patterns in India since independence in 1947. Formal education, media entertainment, and growing population dispersal across the states continue to make the multilingual patterns more dynamic than ever. The country has a wide variety of local languages and, in many cases; the State boundaries have been drawn on linguistic lines. Therefore, the state language of a state, to the majority of the residents, is their mother tongue as well as the most representative local language of the region.

The All India Council for Education recommended the adoption of the Three Language Formula (TLF) in September 1956. The endorsement for this formula came from various directions. It was adopted by the Chief Ministers' conference. The National Policy on Education 1968 recommended the inclusion of the TLF which includes the study of a modern Indian language, preferably one of the Southern languages, apart from Hindi and English in the Hindi speaking states, and of Hindi along with the regional language and English in the non-Hindi speaking states at the Secondary stage. The Three-Language Formula was worked out as a way of accommodating the interest of each linguistic group. The formula is a policy to encourage learner to choose and learn three languages at school. The first one of the three languages, in most cases, is speaker's mother tongue/regional language while the second one is Hindi, a language of national pride and unity. And the last one is English, a language of administrative efficiency, technological progress and international communication.

The NEP 2020 again adopting three language formula, according to this formula, students will be expected to learn at least three languages at school, out of which one will be the local/regional language. The choice of languages learned will depend on the state and student, however, at least two of the three languages must be native to India. The NEP recommends adopting a language policy that integrates an array of regional languages as part of the curriculum at schools and for higher education. The policy celebrates the status quo with some rhetoric added. It is substantially a repetition of the NEPs of 1968 and 1986 (revised 1992) so far as the issues of mother tongue, three-language formula, regional languages, and such languages of power as Hindi and English are concerned. It refuses to look at the National Curriculum Framework (2005) and trivialises both multilingualism and the power of language. NEP 2020 focuses to work on a theoretically grounded pedagogy that treats the languages of learners as a resource and uses them as a platform for acquiring methods of scientific enquiry; we also need to ensure high levels of proficiency in the languages of extant knowledge in a way that leaners are encouraged to not only translate that knowledge into their own languages but also bring to light knowledge systems encoded in their own languages and enrich others with refreshing creativity. The National Education Policy of India 2020 (NEP 2020), designed by the K Kasturirangan Committee, appears to have considered such issues seriously and pragmatically and articulates some novel ideas regarding language teaching. An important object behind the new policy is to make the learners aware of the rich cultural heritage of the nation and to promote multilingualism as well as national unity.

Regarding multilingualism, it can play a significant role in the success of educational policies like the NEP, especially in multicultural and multilingual societies. Here's how:

Access to Opportunities: Multilingualism can provide individuals with access to a broader range of opportunities, including education and employment. Policies under the NEP may aim to uplift marginalized communities, and proficiency in multiple languages can enhance their ability to participate in these opportunities.

Three Language Formula: The three-language formula will continue to be implemented while keeping in mind the Constitutional provisions, the need to promote multilingualism and national unity while providing for greater flexibility. The home/local language and/or the second Indian language will be enhanced with the reading of and analysis of uplifting literature from the Indian subcontinent, ancient to modern, and by authors from all walks of life, as well as through other arts, such as by playing and discussing music or film excerpts, or engaging in theatre in these languages.

Cross-Cultural Communication: In diverse societies, effective communication across linguistic and cultural boundaries is crucial for economic growth. Multilingual individuals can facilitate this communication, helping businesses and policymakers navigate diverse markets and communities more effectively. In cases where home-language textbook material is not available, the language of the transaction between teachers and students will still remain the home language wherever possible. Teachers will be encouraged to use a bilingual approach, including bilingual teaching-learning materials, with those students whose home language may be different from the medium of instruction. All languages will be taught with high quality; a language does not need to be the medium of instruction for it to be learned well.

Workforce Diversity: The NEP may promote diversity and inclusivity in the workforce. Multilingualism enriches this diversity by enabling individuals to engage with colleagues, clients, and stakeholders from different linguistic backgrounds, fostering collaboration and innovation.

Global Competitiveness: In an increasingly interconnected world, multilingualism is an asset for global competitiveness. NEP may seek to enhance a country's competitiveness in the global market, and a multilingual workforce can contribute to this goal by facilitating international trade and diplomacy. The teaching of all languages will be enhanced through innovative and experiential methods, such as gratification and apps, and by weaving in the cultural aspects of the languages, with the teaching-learning of various subjects and with real-life experiences through films, theatre and storytelling, art and music, local literature, etc. Thus, the teaching of languages will also be based on experiential learning pedagogy and this will help students to be prepared for global competitiveness.

However, challenges may also arise in implementing multilingualism within the framework of the NEP:

Resource Allocation: Providing language education and support services for multiple languages can require significant resources. There will be a major effort from both the Central and State governments to invest in large numbers of language teachers in all regional languages around the country. Especially states from different regions of India, may enter bilateral agreements to employ teachers in large numbers from each other, to satisfy the three language formula in their respective states, and also to encourage the study of Indian languages across the countryPolicymakers must balance the benefits of multilingualism with the costs involved, especially in resource-constrained settings.

Language Policy: Developing effective language policies that promote multilingualism while addressing issues of linguistic equity and inclusion can be .complex. Policymakers need to ensure that language policies under the NEP are inclusive and sensitive to linguistic diversity.

Social Cohesion: While multilingualism can enrich societies, it can also pose challenges to social cohesion if not managed properly. In some cases, multilingual individuals may face challenges in social integration, particularly if they belong to linguistic minority groups. They may struggle to find a sense of belonging within monolingual communities. Policies under the NEP should promote linguistic diversity while fostering a sense of belonging and unity among all linguistic communities.

Multilingualism can both complement and present challenges to the implementation of education policies like the NEP. Effective integration of multilingualism within the policy framework requires careful consideration of linguistic diversity, equity, and the socio-economic context. Overall, while multilingualism offers numerous benefits, it also presents challenges that individuals must navigate. Effective language policies and support systems can help maximize the advantages of multilingualism while addressing its potential drawbacks.

References

Baker, C. (2011). *Foundations of Bilingual Education and Bilingualism*. Bristol, UK: Multilingual Matters.

Blackledge, A., & Creese, A. (2010). *Multilingualism, a critical perspective*. London: Continuum.

Bloommaert, J. (2010). *The Sociolinguistics of Globalization*. Cambridge, UK: Cambridge University Press.

Chaudhary, S. (2009). *Foreigners and Foreign Languages in India: A Sociolinguistic History*. New Delhi: Foundation Books, Cambridge University Press.

Chomsky, N. (1986). *Knowledge of Language: Its Nature, Origin, and Use*. New York: Convergence series.

Das Gupta, J. (1970). *Language Conflict and National Development*. Berkeley and Los Angeles: University of California Press.

https://niepid.nic.in/nep_2020.pdf

https://www.education.gov.in/sites/upload_files/mhrd/files/nep_achievement.pdf .

https://www.education.gov.in/sites/upload_files/mhrd/files/NEP_Final_English_0.pdf

Saghal, A. (1991). *Patterns of language use in a bilingual setting in India*. In J. Cheshire, English around the World. Sociolinguistic Perspectives (pp. 299-307). Cambridge: CUP: Cambridge: CUP.

20. Fostering Inclusive Education in India: A Critical Analysis of NEP 2020

Dr. Nirmala S. Padmavat

Introduction

The National Education Policy 2020 (NEP 2020) in India signifies a momentous leap forward in the pursuit of inclusive education, marking a paradigm shift in the educational landscape of the nation. Central to NEP 2020 is the recognition of the pressing need to break down barriers and foster inclusive learning environments that cater to the diverse abilities of all students. By placing inclusivity at the forefront of its agenda, NEP 2020 acknowledges the historical marginalization and exclusion faced by students with diverse needs and commits to rectifying systemic inequities and this policy made drastic changes which are displayed on the internet as The NEP 2020 enacts numerous changes in India's education policy. It aims to increase state expenditure on education from around 3% to 6% of the GDP as soon as possible. The NEP 2020 enacts numerous changes in India's education policy. It aims to increase state expenditure on education from around 3% to 6% of the GDP as soon as possible. Through its comprehensive provisions and policy directives, NEP 2020 seeks to transform educational institutions into spaces where every student, regardless of their background or abilities, feels welcomed, valued, and empowered to thrive. The specific characteristics of NEP 2020 are as below:

Its Emphasis on Inclusivity Reflects a Fundamental Shift in Education

This emphasis on inclusivity reflects a fundamental shift in educational philosophy, prioritizing the principle of equity and affirming the inherent dignity and worth of every individual within the educational ecosystem. As such, NEP 2020 serves as a rallying cry for systemic change, inspiring stakeholders across the educational spectrum to collaborate in the collective endeavor of building a more inclusive and equitable educational system that leaves no student behind.

The Potential Benefits of NEP 2020 in Fostering Empathy

The analysis acknowledges the potential benefits of NEP 2020 in fostering empathy, collaboration, and a heterogeneous learning environment conducive to the holistic development of all students. By emphasizing the inclusion of CWSN in mainstream educational settings, NEP 2020 endeavors to mitigate the marginalization and exclusion historically experienced by this demographic.

The Policy is Emphasis on Personalized Learning Pathways

The policy is emphasis on personalized learning pathways and flexible assessment methodologies holds promise for recognizing and accommodating diverse learning needs. The analysis of the National Education Policy 2020 (NEP 2020) recognizes a myriad of potential benefits that stem from its emphasis on inclusivity, particularly in fostering empathy, collaboration, and the creation of heterogeneous learning environments conducive to the holistic development of all students. By prioritizing inclusivity, NEP 2020 endeavors to cultivate a school culture that celebrates diversity, encourages mutual respect, and nurtures a sense of belonging among students with diverse abilities. Through exposure to peers from varied backgrounds and experiences, students are afforded the opportunity to develop empathy, compassion, and an appreciation for individual differences, essential qualities for fostering inclusive societies in the future.

NEP 2020 Places a Strong Emphasis on the Inclusion of Children with Special Needs

Moreover, NEP 2020 places a strong emphasis on the inclusion of Children with Special Needs (CWSN) in mainstream educational settings, aiming to mitigate the marginalization and exclusion historically experienced by this demographic. By advocating for the integration of CWSN into regular classrooms, NEP 2020 promotes the principles of diversity and inclusion, challenging societal perceptions of disability and affirming the rights of every child to access quality education. Inclusive educational environments not only provide CWSN with equitable learning opportunities but also foster a sense of belonging and acceptance, promoting social integration and reducing the stigma associated with disability. The potential benefits of NEP 2020 in fostering empathy, collaboration, and a heterogeneous learning environment, as well as its emphasis on the inclusion of CWSN and personalized learning pathways, represent significant strides towards creating an inclusive and equitable education system in India. By prioritizing diversity, equity, and inclusion, NEP 2020 lays the foundation for a transformative educational paradigm that affirms the inherent dignity and worth of every student and prepares them to thrive in an increasingly diverse and interconnected world.

NEP 2020's Adoption of Flexible Assessment Methodologies

Adoption of NEP 2020 is flexible assessment methodologies, such as formative assessments, project-based assessments, and competency-based assessments, offers a more holistic and inclusive approach to evaluating student learning. By moving beyond traditional standardized tests, which often fail to capture the diverse talents and capabilities of students, flexible assessment methods provide a more comprehensive picture of student achievement, taking into account factors such as creativity, critical thinking, and problem-solving skills. This shift towards flexible assessment not only reduces the emphasis on rote memorization but also ensures that students with diverse learning needs are given equitable opportunities to demonstrate their knowledge and skills, regardless of their individual challenges or disabilities.

However, amidst these promises lie formidable challenges that impede the effective implementation of inclusive education initiatives outlined in NEP 2020. Chief among these challenges are resource constraints, encompassing financial limitations, inadequate infrastructure, and a shortage of specialized human resources.

Insufficient funding allocations and competing educational priorities often hinder the realization of inclusive education objectives, particularly in resource-constrained settings.

Societal attitudes and ingrained biases also pose significant hurdles to inclusive education. Prevailing stigmas and misconceptions surrounding disability inhibit the creation of truly inclusive learning environments, perpetuating segregation and exclusionary practices. Addressing deep-rooted societal attitudes demands comprehensive awareness campaigns, community engagement initiatives, and advocacy efforts aimed at fostering a culture of inclusivity and acceptance. Moreover, the effective implementation of inclusive education mandates robust monitoring and evaluation mechanisms to assess progress, identify challenges, and inform policy refinements. Ensuring accountability and transparency in the implementation process is essential for driving systemic change and advancing the principles of inclusive education.

SWOC Analysis of NEP 2020

The National Education Policy 2020 (NEP 2020) marks a significant milestone in India's educational journey, aiming to usher in transformative reforms to address the evolving needs of the country's education system. While NEP 2020 has been hailed as a visionary document with the potential to revolutionize education, it is imperative to subject it to critical scrutiny to assess its strengths, weaknesses, opportunities, and threats as below:

Strengths

NEP 2020 introduces several progressive initiatives that hold promise for enhancing the quality, inclusivity, and relevance of education in India. One of its strengths lies in its emphasis on early childhood education and foundational literacy, recognizing the importance of a strong educational foundation in shaping lifelong learning outcomes. The policy's focus on holistic development, including cognitive, social, emotional, and physical aspects, reflects a shift towards a more comprehensive understanding of education. Additionally, NEP 2020's promotion of multidisciplinary education, vocational training, and experiential learning aligns with global best practices and aims to equip students with practical skills for the 21st-century workforce.

Weaknesses

Despite its ambitious vision, NEP 2020 faces several challenges and limitations that may hinder its effective implementation. One of the key weaknesses is the lack of clarity and specificity in certain policy provisions, leaving room for interpretation and potential inconsistencies in implementation. The policy's reliance on decentralized decision-making and autonomy for educational institutions may exacerbate existing disparities and inequities, particularly in resource-constrained regions. Moreover, NEP 2020's ambitious targets and timelines may be unrealistic given the complexities of the Indian education system, raising concerns about feasibility and sustainability.

Opportunities

NEP 2020 presents numerous opportunities for catalyzing positive change and innovation in the education sector. By embracing technology-enabled learning and digital infrastructure, the policy has the potential to expand access to quality education, especially in underserved and remote areas. Furthermore, NEP 2020's emphasis on teacher training and professional development offers an opportunity to enhance the pedagogical skills and competencies of educators, thereby improving instructional quality and student outcomes. Additionally, the policy's recognition of the importance of early childhood education and the integration of vocational training can help bridge the skills gap and foster greater employability among youth.

Threats

Despite its transformative potential, NEP 2020 faces several threats and challenges that may impede its successful implementation. One of the primary threats is the resistance to change from vested interests and entrenched stakeholders within the education system. Resistance from teachers' unions, administrative bureaucracies, and political opposition may undermine the policy's implementation efforts and delay progress. Additionally, the lack of adequate funding and resource allocation poses a significant threat to NEP 2020's ambitious goals, as financial constraints may limit the scope and effectiveness of reform initiatives.

Conclusion

Thus, the National Education Policy 2020 embodies a courageous and forward-thinking endeavor to revolutionize India's education system, aiming to confront enduring obstacles and pave the way for substantive reform. While the policy introduces a host of progressive initiatives and promising opportunities for positive change, it is not immune to the substantial challenges and constraints inherent in its implementation. To navigate these challenges effectively and capitalize on the policy's potential, policymakers, educators, and stakeholders must engage in rigorous critical analysis and scrutiny. By identifying and addressing key areas for improvement, such as clarity in policy provisions, resource allocation, and stakeholder engagement, stakeholders can collectively chart a course towards realizing NEP 2020's transformative vision for education in India. Through concerted efforts and collaborative action, NEP 2020 has the potential to catalyze enduring positive change, ensuring equitable access to quality education and fostering the holistic development of all learners in the country.

References

"*Aishe Ghosh calls internships 'child labour', Twitter mocks 'freeloader communists*'". Free Press Journal. Archived from the original on 6 August 2020. Retrieved 9 August 2020.

"*NEP will transform millions of lives, "says Modi; CPM terms it unilateral drive to destroy education*". Firstpost. 30 July 2020. Archived from the original on 10 August 2020. Retrieved 9 August 2020.

"*NEP 2020 "undermines" Tamil, halts its implementation: Stalin*". The Times of India. PTI. 9 August 2020. Archived from the original on 22 December 2020. Retrieved 9 August 2020.

"*Govt approves plan to boost state spending on education to 6% of GDP*". Livemint. 29 July 2020. Archived from the original on 8 August 2020. Retrieved 30 July 2020.

Stalin, J Sam Daniel (1 June 2019). Dutta Roy, Divyanshu (ed.). "*#Stop Hindi Imposition Protest Erupts Against Centre's Draft Education Plan*". NDTV. Archived from the original on 9 August 2020. Retrieved 30 July 2020.

Sarfaraz, Kainat (29 July 2020). "*Mixed response to new education policy, Sisodia welcomes move to rename MHRD as ministry of education*". Hindustan Times. Archived from the original on 31 July 2020. Retrieved 31 July 2020.

Chaturvedi, Amit (30 July 2020). "*'Much to welcome in National Education Policy but...': Shashi Tharoor highlights some challenges*". Hindustan Times. New Delhi. Archived from the original on 30 July 2020. Retrieved 30 July 2020.

Shukla, Ashish (30 July 2020). "*Netizens irked the Modi government's 3-language formula in NEP 2020*". International Business Times. India. Archived from the original on 9 August 2020. Retrieved 9 August 2020.

Kumar, Shuchita (31 July 2020). "*New education policy: The shift from 10+2 to 5+3+3+4 system*". Times Now. Archived from the original on 11 August 2020. Retrieved 9 August 2020.

Roy, Kumkum (31 July 2020). "*National Education Policy needs close scrutiny for what it says, what it doesn't*". The Indian Express. Archived from the original on 3 August 2020. Retrieved 2 August 2020.

Jain, Sangeet (6 August 2020). "*The National Education Policy 2020: A policy for the times*". ORF. Archived from the original on 23 November 2021. Retrieved 9 August 2020.

21. Advantages, Opportunities and Scope for the Learners in NEP 2020

Dr. Ramakant Dnyanobarao Mundhe

Education is in the real sense, backbone of the human society. We are living in the 21st century where nobody can be survived without education. In the ancient days' people were not literate due to various circumstantial situations. Indian society was under the dominancy of religious authorities and various types of caste based social systems were promoted by the then religious people. Even the king and their kingdom have to follow the decisions given by the religious authorities. As the result of this situation, a few learned people established their hierarchy and keep the entire society under their control and command.

After the Independence of India, education became free for all people. Indian government focused on Education system and provided various educational policies for their countrymen. The present research article will try to focus on the various educational policies run by Government of India. The intention behind this writing is to explore the advantages, opportunities and Scope for the Learners in National Education Policy 2020.

National Education Policy, 2020 (NEP) visualizes a considerable transformation in education through– "an education system rooted in Indian ethos that contributes directly to transforming India, that is Bharat, sustainably into an equitable and vibrant knowledge society, by providing high quality education to all, thereby making India a global knowledge superpower." (https://www.education.gov.in/nep/about-nep) Five guiding pillars considered as the base while preparing the structure of the NEP 2020 are Access, Equity, Quality, Affordability and Accountability. NEP 2020 will assist the young learners of the Nation to cope up with the different national and global challenges of the present and the future.

After the independence of India, since 1947, the government of India paid attention towards the problem of illiteracy throughout the Nation. India's first Education minister, Maulana Abul Kalam Azad, intended that there must be strong control of central government over the National education keeping in mind the uniformity in education. The purpose behind it was that to Indian learner should acquire same knowledge though there was cultural diversity in India. The first action taken to complete this task was, the University Education Commission in1948–1949 was established by The Union government. Various commissions were established like, Secondary Education Commission in1952–1953, University Grants Commission and the Kothari Commission in1964–66 to develop the fundamental education system of modern India. The Government Resolution on Scientific Policy was accepted by the government of India, under the leadership of Pandit Jawaharlal Nehru, India's first Prime Minister. The Indian government promoted various developments of high-quality scientific education institutions like the Indian Institutes of Technology (IIT). The Union government formed the National Council of Educational Research and Training (NCERT) In 1961. As an autonomous organization NCERT has provided full authority to   advise the Union as well as state governments on formulation and implementation education policies.

Later on the government headed by the then Prime Minister Indira Gandhi announced the first National Policy on Education in 1968, Based on the report and recommendations of the Kothari Commission (1964–1966). This Education policy basically focused on the radical restructuring and suggested equal educational opportunities to achieve the national integration and greater cultural and economic development of the Nation. The policy called for fulfilling the mandatory education for the children up to 14 years, as predetermined by the Indian constitution and specific training and qualification of the teachers. The policy focused on the learning of regional languages, emphasizing on the three language formula which would be implemented in secondary education - the instruction of the English language, the official language of the state where the school was based i.e. regional language and Hindi. Language education was the important factor to reduce the gap between the intelligentsia and the masses. As a matter of fact, the decision to accept Hindi as the national language had proven controversial, the policy called for the use and learning of Hindi was encouraged for the uniformly to promote a common language for all Indians. The policy also encouraged the teaching of the ancient and traditional Sanskrit language, which was considered an important part of the Indian culture and the heritage. The National Education Policy of 1968 was framed for the intention for education spending to increase to six percent of the national income of the Nation.

The government led by Rajiv Gandhi implemented new National Policy on Education in the year, 1986. This new education policy specially emphasised on the removal of disparities and to equalise educational opportunity its focus was to provide the education especially to Indian women, Scheduled Caste (SC) and the Scheduled Tribes (ST) communities. To achieve the task of social integration, the National Education Policy suggested starting various scholarships for backward classes, started adult education, more teachers from the SCs were recruited, incentives were given for poor families to send their children to school regularly. The NPE launched, "Operation Blackboard" in primary education keeping in mind the child-centred approach and to improve primary schools all over India. The NEP also expanded the Open University system by starting Indira Gandhi National Open University, in 1985. Rural university model was created, based on Mahatma Gandhi's philosophy, for the sake of social and economic development of lower classes in rural India. 6% of GDP was expected to spend on education in NEP, 1986.

In the year1992, The NEP 1986 on Education was modified in by the P. V. Narasimha Rao government. In the year 2005, the Former Prime Minister of India Dr. Manmohan Singh, the United Progressive Alliance (UPA) government, approved a new policy based on the "Common Minimum Programme". Programme of Action (PoA) 1992, under the National Policy on Education (NPE), 1986 proposed to conduct a common entrance examination on all India level for the admissions of professional and technical programmes in the country. For admission to Engineering and Architecture/Planning programmes, Government of India passed a Resolution on date 18 October 2001 and three mandatory exams were applied those were, (JEE and AIEEE at the National Level and the State Level Engineering Entrance Examinations (SLEEE) for State Level Institutions – with an option to join AIEEE). The due care of varying admission standards in these programmes was taken which helped in maintenance of professional standards. It also solved the problems of overlapping and reduced physical, mental and financial burdens on students and their parents due to multiplicity of entrance examinations.

In the year 2019, the Ministry of Education released a new Draft, New Education Policy 2019, which was followed by a number of public consultations. The NEP-2019, discusses reducing curriculum content to enhance essential learning, critical thinking and more holistic experiential, discussion-based and analysis-based learning. The NEP-2019 talks about a revision of the curriculum and the pedagogical structure from 10+2 system to 5+3+3+4 system design in an effort to rectify learning for students based on analytical development of children. Research Methodology has been added in the last year of graduation course and student has given full choice to leave or to continue the course. In this NEP-2019, the student who will leave the degree class in last year will receive certificate and the student who will complete the graduation will receive degree.

The cabinet approved a new National Education Policy with an aim to introduce several changes to the existing Indian education system On 29 July 2020, which is recognized as NEP-2020, which will be introduced in India till 2026.

In the primary education, the National Education Policy-2020 emphasises on the core values and principle that education must develop not only the analytical skills, the foundational skills of literacy and numeracy and the higher-order skills such as critical thinking and problem solving but also social and emotional skills referred to as soft skills such as perseverance and grit, cultural awareness and empathy, leadership, teamwork, communication, among others. The NEP-2020 directs to globalize the pre-primary education and mainly focuses on the accomplishment of foundational literacy and numeracy in primary school and further on for all by 2025. It recommends plenty of reforms at all levels of school education which seek to ensure quality of schools, transformation of the curriculum including pedagogy with the newly framed 5+3+3+4 design covering children in the age group from 3 to 18 years. NEP-2020 aims to reform in the current examination and assessment system. It will focus on the strengthening of teacher training and also restructuring the education regulatory framework. It aims to increase public investment in education and strengthen the use of technology and increase the focus on vocational and adult education, among others. It suggests that the curriculum load in each subject should be reduced to its core essential content by giving scope for holistic, discussion and analysis-based learning.

NEP-2020, initiates the revision and reconstructing of all aspects of the education structure, along with the school regulation and governance, to create a new system which is aligned with the motivational goals of 21st century education as well as India's tradition, culture and value system. Technology will be combined with education through various existing as well as proposed initiatives, such as high quality e-content for capacity building of teachers and learners, question banks based on learning outcomes, energized text books etc. The policy also points outs that starting primary schools in every habitation across the country have helped in increasing access to education. However, it has led to the development of very small schools with a small number of students which makes it operationally complex to emplace the teachers and the critical physical resources. Hence, the NEP-2020 advocates that multiple public schools can be brought together to form a school complex or any inventive grouping mechanism for effective governance. The policy stresses upon the Quality Education in all stages of School Education. Quality education is life-changing as well as mind-crafting and character-building experience which positively impacts on the citizenship. Empowered learners will contribute in many growing developmental imperatives of the country as well as participate in creating a just and equitable society.

In Higher Education, NEP- 2020 contributes valuable insights and recommendations on different aspects of education which includes institutional autonomy, moving towards multidisciplinary and holistic education, promotion of quality research through establishment of National Research Foundation, integration of technology, continuous professional development of teachers, restructuring of governance and regulatory architecture, internationalization of higher education, multidisciplinary curricula, engaging blended, pedagogy, valid reliable and blended assessment and availability of content in Indian languages. The policy is intending to bring permanent positive impact on the education system which would make India a global hub of skilled manpower during the 'Amrit Kaal' i.e. the golden era, the next 25 years leading up to Developed India in 2047. All the governing bodies of

Centre, States, UTs, HEIs, Regulating Agencies   and all other relevant stakeholders must have to make collective efforts for the implementation of NEP-2020.

References

https://www.education.gov.in/nep/about-nep

https://en.wikipedia.org/wiki/National_Policy_on_Education#cite_note-NCERT-2

https://en.wikipedia.org/wiki/Secondary_Education_Commission

https://en.wikipedia.org/wiki/Constitution_of_India

https://en.wikipedia.org/wiki/Intelligentsia

https://en.wikipedia.org/wiki/National_Policy_on_Education#cite_note-B-4

https://en.wikipedia.org/wiki/Open_university_(concept)

https://en.wikipedia.org/wiki/National_Policy_on_Education#cite_note-A501-7

https://en.wikipedia.org/wiki/Mahatma_Gandhi

https://en.wikipedia.org/wiki/National_Policy_on_Education#cite_note-8

https://en.wikipedia.org/wiki/P._V._Narasimha_Rao

https://en.wikipedia.org/wiki/United_Progressive_Alliance

https://en.wikipedia.org/wiki/Manmohan_Singh

https://en.wikipedia.org/wiki/National_Policy_on_Education#cite_note-11

22. Tech-Driven Transformation: Exploring the Intersection of National Education Policy and English Language Teaching for Inclusive and Innovative Learning Experiences

Durva Kishor Mandrekar

The National Education Policy (NEP) of India, introduced in 2020, embodies a comprehensive vision for reforming the country's education system. At its core, the NEP aims to address longstanding challenges and inequities while promoting inclusive, high-quality education for all. Central to this vision is the recognition of technology as a powerful enabler of educational transformation. By emphasizing the integration of technology across all levels of education, the NEP seeks to harness its potential to enhance learning outcomes, expand access to educational resources, and foster innovation in teaching and learning practices.

Within the NEP, technology integration is envisioned as a means to democratize access to education, bridging geographical and socio-economic divides. Digital platforms and online resources offer learners unprecedented access to a diverse range of educational materials, including multimedia content, interactive exercises, and virtual classrooms. This expanded access to resources can be particularly beneficial for English language learners, providing them with immersive language experiences and authentic language use opportunities that transcend traditional classroom boundaries.

Moreover, the NEP emphasizes the importance of digital literacy and fluency, recognizing them as essential skills for navigating an increasingly digital world. By equipping students with the knowledge and skills to leverage technology effectively, the NEP aims to empower them to become lifelong learners and active participants in the digital economy. For English language learners, this includes not only proficiency in using digital tools but also the ability to critically evaluate and engage with digital content in English.

In addition to expanding access and promoting digital literacy, the NEP encourages the integration of technology to personalize learning experiences and support individualized instruction. Adaptive learning platforms, AI-powered language learning tools, and data-driven insights enable educators to tailor instruction to meet the diverse needs and learning styles of students. This personalized approach can be particularly impactful for English language teaching, where learners may have varying levels of proficiency and language backgrounds.

Technology plays a pivotal role in enhancing English language teaching by providing educators and learners with a plethora of tools and resources to facilitate language acquisition. One of the primary advantages of technology-enhanced learning is the ability to cater to diverse learning styles and preferences. Through the integration of multimedia resources, such as videos, audio recordings, interactive games, and digital textbooks, learners can engage with language content in dynamic and interactive ways. These multimedia resources not only make learning more enjoyable and engaging but also facilitate comprehension and retention of language concepts through visual and auditory stimuli.

Online platforms further augment the learning experience by providing learners with access to a wide range of authentic language materials and resources. From virtual libraries and digital archives to language learning apps and social media platforms, online resources offer learners opportunities for independent study, authentic language use, and cultural immersion. Additionally, online platforms enable learners to connect with peers and language speakers from around the world, fostering collaboration, communication, and intercultural competence.

Moreover, the advent of AI-powered language learning tools has revolutionized the way English language teaching is conducted. These tools utilize artificial intelligence and machine learning algorithms to personalize instruction, provide feedback, and track learners' progress. Adaptive learning platforms, for example, can tailor instruction to meet the individual needs and proficiency levels of learners, offering targeted exercises and interventions based on learners' strengths and weaknesses.

AI-powered chatbots and virtual tutors simulate real-life conversational interactions, providing learners with opportunities to practice speaking and listening skills in a supportive and non-judgmental environment.

Personalized learning experiences have emerged as a cornerstone of effective English language teaching, as they allow educators to tailor instruction to the unique needs, interests, and learning styles of individual learners. By recognizing and accommodating the diverse backgrounds, proficiency levels, and learning preferences of students, personalized learning approaches aim to optimize learning outcomes and engagement. In the context of English language teaching, personalized instruction may involve adapting curriculum materials, instructional strategies, and assessment methods to meet the specific needs and goals of learners. For example, educators may differentiate instruction based on learners' language proficiency levels, providing additional support or challenges as needed, or incorporating culturally relevant content to enhance relevance and engagement.

Adaptive learning platforms represent a key technological innovation in personalized language learning, offering dynamic and adaptive instruction that adjusts in real-time based on learners' responses and performance. These platforms leverage data analytics and machine learning algorithms to assess learners' strengths and weaknesses, identify learning gaps, and deliver targeted interventions and resources accordingly. For English language learners, adaptive learning platforms offer several benefits, including personalized pacing, customized content, and immediate feedback. Learners can progress at their own pace, revisiting concepts or skills as needed, while receiving personalized recommendations for further study or practice.

The benefits of personalized learning experiences for English language learners are manifold. Firstly, personalized instruction addresses the diverse needs and proficiency levels of learners, ensuring that each student receives the support and scaffolding necessary to progress in their language learning journey. Secondly, personalized learning approaches promote learner autonomy and agency, empowering students to take ownership of their learning and pursue their individual language learning goals. Additionally, personalized instruction fosters a positive learning environment characterized by mutual respect, collaboration, and trust, as educators and learners work together to co-create meaningful and relevant learning experiences.

Moreover, personalized learning experiences enhance motivation and engagement among English language learners by catering to their interests, preferences, and learning styles. By aligning instruction with learners' interests and aspirations, educators can foster intrinsic motivation and a sense of purpose, leading to increased engagement, perseverance, and achievement. Furthermore, personalized learning approaches facilitate the development of critical thinking skills, problem-solving abilities, and metacognitive strategies, as learners are encouraged to reflect on their learning processes, set goals, and monitor their progress. Overall, personalized learning experiences hold great promise for optimizing English language teaching and learning outcomes, empowering learners to become proficient, confident, and lifelong language users.

Collaboration and communication skills development are essential components of effective English language teaching, and technology plays a crucial role in facilitating these aspects of language learning. By leveraging technology for collaborative activities, educators can create engaging and interactive learning experiences that promote collaboration, communication, and teamwork among learners. Online platforms and digital tools offer a wide range of opportunities for learners to work together on projects, exchange ideas, and collaborate on tasks in real-time. For example, collaborative document editing tools allow students to collaborate on writing assignments, providing feedback and suggestions to each other, while virtual discussion forums and chat rooms enable asynchronous communication and collaboration outside of the classroom.

Virtual classrooms represent another important technological innovation that supports collaboration and communication skills development in English language teaching. Virtual classroom platforms provide educators with the ability to conduct live, interactive lessons in an online environment, allowing learners to participate in discussions, ask questions, and engage with course materials in real-time. Through features such as video conferencing, screen sharing, and interactive whiteboards, virtual classrooms facilitate dynamic and engaging interactions between educators and learners, as well as among peers.

Moreover, virtual classrooms offer opportunities for learners to practice and develop their speaking and listening skills in a supportive and interactive environment, fostering confidence and fluency in English communication.

Communication tools, such as video conferencing apps, instant messaging platforms, and social media networks, also play a crucial role in supporting collaboration and communication skills development in English language teaching. These tools enable learners to engage in real-time communication with peers and language speakers from around the world, providing authentic language use opportunities and cultural exchange experiences. Through virtual language exchanges, online language learning communities, and collaborative projects with learners from diverse backgrounds, students can develop their speaking, listening, and intercultural communication skills in authentic and meaningful contexts. Additionally, communication tools allow educators to provide timely feedback, facilitate discussions, and promote active participation in the language learning process, fostering a supportive and communicative learning environment.

The literature on the effectiveness of technology integration in language learning provides valuable insights into its impact on learners' proficiency, engagement, and motivation. Numerous studies have explored the benefits of incorporating technology into language teaching and learning, highlighting its potential to enhance language acquisition and promote meaningful interaction with language content. For example, research has shown that multimedia resources, such as videos, audio recordings, and interactive games, can increase learners' exposure to authentic language input and improve their comprehension skills. Similarly, online platforms and digital tools offer opportunities for self-directed learning, collaboration, and real-world language use, leading to improvements in speaking, listening, reading, and writing skills.

Additionally, case studies of successful implementation shed light on effective strategies and best practices for integrating technology into language learning contexts. These case studies often highlight innovative approaches and pedagogical strategies that leverage technology to create engaging and interactive learning experiences. For instance, successful implementations may involve the use of virtual reality simulations for immersive language practice, mobile apps for vocabulary acquisition, or social media platforms for authentic communication and cultural exchange. By examining these case studies, educators can gain valuable insights into how technology can be effectively integrated into language teaching and learning to maximize learning outcomes.

Despite the potential benefits of technology integration, challenges and barriers exist that may hinder its effective implementation in language learning contexts. Common challenges identified in research include issues related to digital infrastructure and access, technological literacy and training, and pedagogical integration. For instance, learners from disadvantaged backgrounds may lack access to reliable internet connectivity or digital devices, limiting their ability to participate in technology-enhanced learning activities. Similarly, educators may face challenges in selecting appropriate technology tools and resources, integrating them into existing curriculum and pedagogy, and addressing technical issues or resistance to change among students or colleagues.

Moreover, concerns about the quality and effectiveness of technology-enhanced learning resources, data privacy and security, and digital distractions are also raised in the literature. Addressing these challenges requires careful planning, collaboration, and ongoing support from policymakers, administrators, educators, and technology developers. By identifying and addressing these challenges, educators can harness the full potential of technology to enhance language teaching and learning and prepare learners for success in an increasingly digital and interconnected world.

Effective integration of technology into language teaching requires a comprehensive approach that encompasses teacher training and professional development, curriculum design, and the selection of appropriate technology tools and resources. Teacher training and professional development programs play a crucial role in equipping educators with the knowledge, skills, and confidence needed to effectively integrate technology into their teaching practices. These programs should focus on familiarizing educators with a range of technology tools and platforms, demonstrating best practices for their use in language teaching, and providing ongoing support and mentoring opportunities. By investing in teacher training and professional development, institutions can empower educators to leverage technology to enhance learning outcomes and meet the diverse needs of learners.

Curriculum design and lesson planning are essential components of effective technology integration in language teaching. Educators must align technology-enhanced activities and resources with curriculum standards, learning objectives, and language proficiency goals. This involves careful consideration of the types of technology tools and resources that best support language learning objectives and promote meaningful language use. Additionally, educators should design lessons that incorporate a variety of technology tools and resources to engage learners, accommodate diverse learning styles, and address different language skills. By integrating technology into curriculum design and lesson planning, educators can create dynamic and interactive learning experiences that foster student engagement and promote language learning outcomes.

Selecting appropriate technology tools and resources is crucial for successful integration into language teaching. Educators must carefully evaluate and choose tools that best meet the needs and goals of their teaching context. Factors such as ease of use, compatibility with existing infrastructure, suitability for language learning objectives, and alignment with pedagogical approaches should be considered when selecting technology tools. Additionally, educators should assess the quality, relevance, and effectiveness of digital resources, such as multimedia materials, online platforms, and language learning apps, to ensure they support language proficiency development and promote authentic language use. By selecting appropriate technology tools and resources, educators can optimize the integration of technology into language teaching and maximize its impact on student learning.

Considerations for implementing technology integration in language teaching encompass a range of factors aimed at ensuring equitable access, effective implementation, and cultural relevance. One critical consideration is addressing access to technology and mitigating digital divide issues. It is imperative to ensure that all learners, regardless of socioeconomic status or geographical location, have access to the necessary technology tools and resources. This may involve providing loaner devices, subsidizing internet access, or leveraging community resources to bridge the gap in access. Additionally, educators should be mindful of learners' varying levels of technological proficiency and provide support as needed to ensure equitable participation.

Furthermore, infrastructure requirements must be carefully considered to support technology-enhanced language teaching initiatives. Educational institutions need to invest in adequate hardware, software, and networking capabilities to facilitate seamless integration of technology into teaching and learning activities. This includes upgrading computer labs, installing Wi-Fi networks, and ensuring sufficient bandwidth to support online learning. Additionally, the availability of technical support and maintenance services is essential to address any technical issues that may arise during implementation.

Moreover, cultural and contextual factors play a crucial role in shaping the effectiveness and appropriateness of technology integration in language teaching. Educators must consider learners' cultural backgrounds, linguistic diversity, and educational experiences when selecting technology tools and designing learning activities. Digital resources and content should be culturally relevant and sensitive to learners' identities, and instructional strategies should align with cultural norms and expectations regarding technology use in educational settings. By incorporating cultural and contextual factors into technology integration initiatives, educators can ensure that technology-enhanced language teaching is culturally responsive, inclusive, and effective for all learners. Addressing these considerations is essential for successful implementation and maximizing the benefits of technology in language teaching and learning.

Best practices in technology integration in English language classrooms often involve innovative approaches and pedagogical strategies that leverage technology to enhance language learning outcomes. One successful model of technology integration is the flipped classroom approach, where traditional lecture content is delivered online outside of class, allowing for more interactive and hands-on activities during class time. In English language classrooms, this may involve assigning multimedia resources, such as videos or interactive tutorials, for students to review before class, followed by in-class activities such as group discussions, collaborative projects, or language practice exercises. This approach promotes active learning, student engagement, and personalized instruction, as educators can use class time to provide targeted support and feedback to individual learners.

Innovative approaches and pedagogical strategies that leverage technology include the use of digital storytelling, gamification, and project-based learning. Digital storytelling allows students to create and share multimedia narratives using digital tools such as video editors, audio recording software, or storytelling apps. This approach fosters creativity, critical thinking, and language expression, as students engage in the process of writing, editing, and presenting their own stories in English. Similarly, gamification involves incorporating game elements, such as points, levels, and rewards, into language learning activities to increase motivation, engagement, and retention of language content. For example, language learning apps and platforms may use gamified features such as quizzes, challenges, and leaderboards to encourage learners to practice vocabulary, grammar, and pronunciation skills in a fun and interactive way.

Lessons learned from implementation experiences in technology integration highlight the importance of careful planning, ongoing support, and flexibility in adapting to learners' needs and preferences. Educators should take a learner-centered approach to technology integration, considering learners' interests, motivations, and learning styles when selecting technology tools and designing learning activities. Additionally, providing ongoing training, technical support, and opportunities for collaboration and peer learning can help educators build confidence and expertise in using technology effectively in their teaching practice. Furthermore, educators should be flexible and willing to adapt their instructional strategies based on feedback from students, monitoring student progress, and adjusting the pace and content of instruction as needed to ensure that technology-enhanced learning experiences are engaging, relevant, and effective for all learners. By reflecting on lessons learned from implementation experiences and incorporating best practices and innovative approaches into their teaching, educators can maximize the benefits of technology integration in English language classrooms and enhance language learning outcomes for their students.

Aligning technology integration with the goals outlined in the National Education Policy (NEP) of India is essential for driving education reform and achieving the policy's vision of inclusive, equitable, and high-quality education for all. Technology plays a critical role in supporting the NEP's vision for education reform by democratizing access to education, promoting digital literacy, and fostering innovation in teaching and learning practices. By leveraging technology, educators can create dynamic and interactive learning experiences that cater to diverse learner needs and preferences, thereby promoting student engagement, motivation, and achievement. Additionally, technology-enabled learning platforms and resources offer opportunities for self-directed learning, collaboration, and real-world application of knowledge, aligning with the NEP's emphasis on developing critical thinking, creativity, and problem-solving skills among learners. By integrating technology into education practices in alignment with the NEP's goals, educators can create a more inclusive, flexible, and responsive learning environment that empowers learners to succeed in an increasingly digital and interconnected world.

Furthermore, leveraging technology can enhance inclusivity and access to education, addressing disparities in educational opportunities and outcomes among learners. By providing learners with access to digital resources and online learning platforms, technology bridges geographical and socio-economic divides, enabling learners from diverse backgrounds to access high-quality educational materials and opportunities. Additionally, adaptive learning platforms and personalized learning experiences cater to individual learner needs, ensuring that every student receives the support and scaffolding necessary to succeed. Moreover, technology-enabled communication tools facilitate collaboration and cultural exchange among learners, promoting diversity, equity, and inclusion in the learning process. By leveraging technology to enhance inclusivity and access, educators can advance the NEP's goals of promoting equity, social justice, and equal opportunities for all learners, regardless of their background or circumstances.

Meeting the challenges and opportunities outlined in the NEP requires a concerted effort to address the complexities and nuances of technology integration in education. Educators must navigate challenges such as digital infrastructure gaps, technological literacy, and pedagogical integration to ensure that technology enhances, rather than detracts from, the quality and effectiveness of education. Additionally, educators should leverage opportunities for innovation, collaboration, and professional development to maximize the benefits of technology in education. By embracing a learner-centered approach to technology integration and fostering a culture of continuous improvement and adaptation, educators can overcome challenges and capitalize on opportunities to transform education in alignment with the NEP's vision. Through strategic planning, collaboration, and ongoing support, technology integration can play a pivotal role in advancing education reform and realizing the NEP's goals of promoting equity, excellence, and inclusivity in education.

In conclusion, the integration of technology into English language teaching offers numerous benefits, including enhanced engagement, personalized learning experiences, and increased access to educational resources. Through a comprehensive review of the literature, it is evident that technology has the potential to transform language learning outcomes and support the goals outlined in the National Education Policy (NEP) of India. By leveraging technology, educators can create dynamic and interactive learning experiences that cater to diverse learner needs, promote collaboration and communication skills, and enhance inclusivity and access to education. However, the effective integration of technology requires careful planning, ongoing support, and alignment with pedagogical goals and curriculum objectives.

Moving forward, policymakers, educators, and researchers must collaborate to harness the full potential of technology in English language teaching within the framework of the NEP. Recommendations for policymakers include investing in digital infrastructure, providing funding for technology integration initiatives, and establishing guidelines and standards for the effective use of technology in education. For educators, ongoing professional development and training are essential to build confidence and expertise in using technology effectively in their teaching practice. Additionally, educators should adopt a learner-centered approach to technology integration, considering learners' needs, preferences, and cultural backgrounds when selecting technology tools and designing learning activities.

Furthermore, there are several areas for further research and exploration to advance technology-enhanced English language teaching within the framework of the NEP. Future research could focus on investigating the impact of specific technology tools and resources on language learning outcomes, exploring innovative pedagogical approaches and best practices for technology integration, and examining the effectiveness of different models of professional development and training for educators. Additionally, research could explore the potential of emerging technologies, such as artificial intelligence, virtual reality, and augmented reality, to enhance language learning experiences and support the goals of the NEP.

Technology integration holds great promise for transforming English language teaching and advancing education reform in India. By aligning technology integration initiatives with the goals outlined in the NEP and prioritizing collaboration, innovation, and research, policymakers, educators, and researchers can work together to create inclusive, equitable, and high-quality learning opportunities for all learners.

References

Aithal, P. S., and Shubhrajyotsna Aithal. *"Analysis of the Indian National Education Policy 2020 Towards Achieving Its Objectives."* International Journal of Management, Technology, and Social Science, Aug. 2020, pp. 19–41. https://doi.org/10.47992/ijmts.2581.6012.0102.

Aithal, Sreeramana, and Shubhrajyotsna Aithal. *"Analysis of Higher Education in Indian National Education Policy Proposal 2019 and Its Implementation Challenges."* International Journal of Applied Engineering and Management Letters, Nov. 2019, pp. 1–35. https://doi.org/10.47992/ijaeml.2581.7000.0039.

Pendor, Sujata Mohan. *"NEP 2020 Use of Technology in Education."* Sumedha Journal of Management, vol. 11, no. 3, May 2022, https://doi.org/10.46454/sumedha/11.3.2022.442.

Erben, Tony, et al. *Teaching English Language Learners Through Technology.* 2008, tesol-dev.journals.cdrs.columbia.edu/wp-content/uploads/sites/12/2015/06/5.-Madrazo-2010.pdf.

23. The Intersection of Music Therapy and Artificial Intelligence: Applications and Challenges

Satish Mekewad, Santosh Khamitkar, Sakharam Lokhande & Parag Bhalchandra

Introduction

Music therapy has been recognized for its therapeutic effects on mental health, encompassing interventions such as receptive music listening, active music-making, and improvisation. While traditional music therapy approaches have shown efficacy, recent advancements in AI present new possibilities for enhancing therapeutic outcomes and accessibility. As of last update in January 2022, music therapy in India has been gaining recognition and acceptance as a complementary approach to conventional medical treatment. Music therapy is the clinical and evidence-based use of music interventions to accomplish individualized goals within a therapeutic relationship by a credentialed professional. While it's not as widely established as in some Western countries, there has been a growing interest in integrating music therapy into healthcare practices in India. The study identified a gap in the smart home market and proposed an adaptive system combining music therapy and AI technology. Music, personalized to users' needs, could serve as a substitute for anxiety and depression medication. The system interacts through speakers and an app, offering holistic support for mental well-being [1]. A meta-analysis by [2] demonstrated the effectiveness of music therapy in reducing symptoms of depression. A study by [3] found that music therapy was effective in reducing symptoms of anxiety in adult psychiatric patients. A randomized controlled trial by [4] showed that group improvisational music therapy was effective in reducing symptoms of depression in adults with depression. This paper examines the intersection of music therapy and AI, exploring how AI-driven approaches can optimize personalized interventions and improve mental well-being.

Literature review and current status of music therapy in India

Music therapy encompasses a range of interventions tailored to individual needs, with evidence supporting its effectiveness in improving mood, reducing anxiety, and enhancing overall well-being [5,6]. Recent advancements in AI technology have facilitated the development of innovative applications in music therapy. Machine learning algorithms can analyze musical features and emotional responses, enabling personalized music recommendations and adaptive interventions [7,8]. AI-driven systems can analyze user preferences, emotional states, and physiological data to tailor music therapy interventions to individual needs [9]. By providing personalized music selections and therapeutic activities, AI enhances engagement and efficacy in music therapy sessions. AI algorithms can provide real-time feedback during music therapy sessions, adjusting music parameters based on user responses and emotional cues [10]. This real-time adaptation enhances the therapeutic experience and promotes emotional regulation. The integration of AI in music therapy raises ethical concerns regarding privacy, data security, and algorithmic bias [11]. It is essential to develop ethical guidelines and regulatory frameworks to ensure responsible use of AI technologies in mental health care. While AI augments the practice of music therapy, human therapists play a crucial role in establishing rapport, providing emotional support, and interpreting non-verbal cues [12]. Human-AI collaboration is necessary to optimize therapeutic outcomes while preserving the human touch in therapy.

In India, music therapy is gaining recognition as an effective approach for addressing mental health issues. Organizations such as the Indian Music Therapy Association (IMTA) are working to promote the integration of music therapy into clinical practice and educational settings [13]. However, the field is still in its nascent stages, and there is a need for greater awareness, training programs, and research initiatives to advance music therapy in India. The use of music as a therapeutic tool has deep roots in Indian culture, with ancient texts such as the Vedas mentioning the healing power of music [14]. Traditional Indian music forms such as classical music, bhajans, and ragas have been used for centuries to evoke specific emotions and promote well-being [15]. In recent years, there has been a growing interest in Western music therapy approaches in India, with several institutions offering training programs and workshops in music therapy [16]. Additionally, research studies conducted in India have explored the effectiveness of music therapy interventions for various populations, including children with autism spectrum disorder (ASD) and individuals with mental health disorders [17,18].

Despite these developments, challenges such as limited awareness among healthcare professionals, lack of standardized training programs, and insufficient research funding continue to hinder the widespread adoption of music therapy in India. However, with increasing recognition of the importance of mental health and well-being, there is growing momentum to integrate music therapy into mainstream healthcare services and educational institutions across the country.

Growing Precognition: Over the past decade, there has been an increased recognition of the benefits of music therapy among healthcare professionals, educators, and the general public in India. This recognition has led to the integration of music therapy programs in various healthcare settings, educational institutions, and community centers.

Training Programs: Several institutions in India now offer training and certification programs in music therapy. These programs are designed to equip individuals with the knowledge and skills needed to practice music therapy effectively. However, compared to some Western countries, the number of certified music therapists in India is relatively small [13,16].

Applications in healthcare: Music therapy is being used in a variety of healthcare settings in India, including hospitals, rehabilitation centers, psychiatric facilities, and palliative care units. It is employed to address a wide range of physical, emotional, cognitive, and social needs in patients of all ages [17,19].

Research and evidence: While there is growing anecdotal evidence supporting the efficacy of music therapy in India, there is still a need for more systematic research to establish its effectiveness across different populations and clinical conditions. Efforts are being made to conduct research studies and clinical trials to generate more robust evidence [18,20].

Challenges: Despite the progress, music therapy in India faces several challenges, including a lack of awareness among the general public and healthcare professionals, limited funding and resources for research and training programs, and the need for greater standardization and regulation of practice [21,22].

Music Therapy for Anxiety and Depression

Evidence Supporting Music Therapy, Mechanism of Action and Practical Applications:

Anxiety Reduction: Numerous studies have demonstrated the efficacy of music therapy in reducing symptoms of anxiety. For example, a meta-analysis by [23] found that music interventions significantly decreased anxiety levels across various populations.

Depression Management: Music therapy has also shown promise in managing symptoms of depression. A systematic review by [24] reported positive effects of music therapy on mood and depressive symptoms in individuals with depression.

Emotional Regulation: Music has the ability to evoke and regulate emotions, providing a non-verbal outlet for individuals to express and process their feelings [25].

Neurobiological Effects: Listening to music stimulates various brain regions associated with emotion processing and reward, leading to mood enhancement and stress reduction [26].

Individual Sessions: Music therapists tailor interventions to individuals' preferences and therapeutic goals, using techniques such as guided imagery, improvisation, and lyric analysis to address anxiety and depression [4].

Group Therapy: Group music therapy sessions provide opportunities for social interaction, peer support, and shared musical experiences, contributing to a sense of belonging and emotional well-being [27].

AI and Music Therapy

Artificial Intelligence (AI) is revolutionizing various fields of healthcare, including mental health interventions. One area of interest is its integration with music therapy, offering personalized and adaptive interventions for individuals experiencing mental health challenges. This paper explores the advancements, applications, and challenges of incorporating AI into music therapy practices.

Its Advancements, Applications and Challenges of AI in Music Therapy

Personalized Interventions: AI algorithms can analyze individual preferences, emotional states, and physiological data to tailor music therapy interventions to specific needs [9].

Real-time Feedback and Adaptation: AI-powered systems provide real-time feedback during therapy sessions, adjusting music parameters based on user responses and emotional cues [10].

Emotion Precognition: AI algorithms can analyze facial expressions, tone of voice, and other physiological indicators to assess users' emotional states and select appropriate music interventions [7].

Music Composition and Generation: AI technologies enable the creation of personalized music compositions tailored to individuals' therapeutic needs and preferences [8].

Ethical Concerns: The use of AI in music therapy raises ethical questions regarding privacy, data security, and algorithmic bias, necessitating the development of ethical guidelines and regulatory frameworks [11].

Human-AI Collaborations: While AI augments music therapy practices, human therapists play a crucial role in establishing rapport, providing emotional support, and interpreting non-verbal cues, highlighting the importance of human-AI collaboration [12].

EEG headband, AI and Music Therapy

EEG headband technology combined with Artificial Intelligence (AI) has emerged as a novel approach to enhance personalized interventions in music therapy. By leveraging real-time brainwave data and AI algorithms, this integrated system offers tailored therapeutic experiences for individuals with diverse mental health needs. This paper explores the potential applications, benefits, and challenges of utilizing EEG headbands and AI in music therapy.

Its Applications, Benefits of Integration and Challenges

Brainwave Analysis: EEG headbands capture neural activity in real-time, providing insights into users' cognitive and emotional states during music therapy sessions [28].

Emotions Recognition: AI algorithms analyze EEG data to identify patterns associated with different emotional states, enabling the selection of music interventions tailored to individuals' emotional needs [29].

Personalized Interventions: EEG-AI systems allow for precise customization of music therapy interventions based on users' neural responses, enhancing therapeutic outcomes and user engagement [30].

Real-time FeedBack: By providing real-time feedback on users' brainwave patterns, EEG-AI systems facilitate adaptive adjustments to music parameters, optimizing the therapeutic process [31].

Data Security and Privacy: EEG data collection raises concerns about data security and privacy, necessitating robust encryption protocols and adherence to ethical guidelines [32].

Interpretation of EEG Signals: Accurate interpretation of EEG signals requires expertise in neuroscience and signal processing, highlighting the importance of interdisciplinary collaboration in developing EEG-AI systems for music therapy [33].

Conclusion

The music therapy is still in the early stages of development in India, there is a growing interest and momentum behind its integration into healthcare and allied fields. With continued advocacy, research, and education, it is expected to play a more significant role in improving the health and well-being of individuals across the country. While AI holds great promise for enhancing music therapy, it's important to recognize the ethical implications and potential limitations of AI-driven interventions. Therapists must ensure that AI technologies are used responsibly, ethically, and in ways that prioritize the well-being and autonomy of their clients. Additionally, human expertise and empathy remain essential in the therapeutic process, and AI should be seen as a supportive tool rather than a replacement for human interaction.

The integration of EEG headbands with AI technology represents a groundbreaking development in the field of music therapy, enabling personalized, data-driven interventions that harness the power of neuroplasticity to promote healing and well-being. However, it's essential to ensure that ethical considerations, such as privacy and informed consent, are carefully addressed in the development and implementation of EEG-based AI applications in music therapy.

References

Aalbers, S., Fusar-Poli, L., Freeman, R. E., Spreen, M., Ket, J. C., Vink, A. C., ... & van Steenbergen, H. (2017). *Music therapy for depression*. Cochrane Databse of Systematic Review, 11, CD004517.

Ang, K. K. (2019). *EEG-based personalized music recommendation system*. IEEE Access, 7, 51722-51730.

Bhat, S. S., & Rao, P. K. (2017). *Effectiveness of music therapy on depression among mentally ill patients in a selected psychiatric hospital at Mangalore*. International Journal of Nursing Education, 9(2), 126-130.

Dias, B. M., Romano, D. M., Silva, L. A., & Júnior, L. C. (2020). *Artificial intelligence in music therapy: Literature review*. Anais do Congresso Internacional de Educação e Tecnologia, 3(1), 397-407.

Dignum, V., Villata, S., Rodríguez-Aguilar, J. A., & Morel, S. (2020). *Ethical considerations of AI in music therapy*. In Proceedings of the 19th International Conference on Autonomous Agents and MultiAgent Systems (pp. 2717-2719).

Erkkilä, J., Punkanen, M., Fachner, J., Ala-Ruona, E., Pöntiö, I., Tervaniemi, M., ... & Gold, C. (2011). *Individual music therapy for depression: randomised controlled trial*. The British Journal of Psychiatry, 199(2), 132-139.

Gadhavi, P. P., & Pancholi, V. (2019). *The impact of music therapy on anxiety and depression in patients with cancer*. Indian Journal of Palliative Care, 25(1), 36-41.

Gerber, N., Jentschke, S., & King, A. (2018). *Artificial intelligence and the future of music therapy*. Music Therapy Perspectives, 36(2), 226-233.

Gold, C., Solli, H. P., Krüger, V., Lie, S. A., & Doseki, T. (2019). *Music therapy for mental health problems: A systematic review and meta-analysis.* Nordic Journal of Music Therapy, 28 (4), 292-315.

Gold, C., Voracek, M., & Wigram, T. (2004). *Effects of music therapy for children and adolescents with psychopathology: A meta-analysis.* Journal of Child Psychology and Psychiatry, 45(6), 1054-1063.

Indian Music Therapy Association. (n.d.). Retrieved from https://www.indianmusictherapyassociation.com/

Koelsch, S. (2014). *Brain correlates of music-evoked emotions.* Nature Reviews Neuroscience, 15(3), 170-180.

Kumar, M., et al. (2021). *Adaptive emotional music recommendation system based on EEG signals.* Cognitive Neurodynamics, 15(2), 255-267.

Lin, C. T., et al. (2020). *A real-time EEG-based music generation system integrated with emotion recognition.* Journal of Neuroscience Methods, 339, 108733.

López-Larraz, E., et al. (2018). *Brain-machine interfaces for rehabilitation in stroke: A review.* NeuroRehabilitation,43 (1), 77-97.

Maratos, A. S., Gold, C., Wang, X., & Crawford, M. J. (2008). *Music therapy for depression.* Cochrane Databse of Systematic Review, 11, CD004517.

Maratos, A., Gold, C., Wang, X., & Crawford, M. (2008). *Music therapy for depression.* Cochrane Database of Systematic Reviews, 2008(1).

Mcdermott, Dustin, and Byungsoo Kim. "*Artificail Intelligence, Music Therapy, And The Fight Against Mental Illness.*"

McDonnell, M. D., et al. (2019). *Applications and limitations of machine learning in human brain decoding.* Nature Reviews Neuroscience,20 (4), 231-245.

McKinney, M. F., & Moelants, D. (2019). *Introduction to computer-based music analysis.* In The Routledge Companion to Music Cognition (pp. 191-204). Routledge.

Nehru Arts and Science College. (n.d.). Certificate course in music therapy. Retrieved from https://nehruartscollege.ac.in/

Pandey, M. (2019). *Music therapy in ancient Indian texts: Vedic roots and evolution.* International Journal of Indian Psychology, 7(3), 1164-1173.

Paszke, A., Gross, S., Massa, F., Lerer, A., Bradbury, J., Chanan, G., ... & Chintala, S. (2019). *PyTorch: An imperative style, high-performance deep learning library.* In Advances in Neural Information Processing Systems (pp. 8024-8035).

Salimpoor, V. N., Benovoy, M., Larcher, K., Dagher, A., & Zatorre, R. J. (2015). *Anatomically distinct dopamine release during anticipation and experience of peak emotion to music.* Nature Neuroscience, 14(2), 257-262.

Särkämö, T., Tervaniemi, M., Laitinen, S., Forsblom, A., Soinila, S., Mikkonen, M., ... & Hietanen, M. (2014). *Music listening enhances cognitive recovery and mood after stroke: a randomized controlled trial.* Journal of Music Therapy, 51(2), 281-299.

Schäfer, T., Sedlmeier, P., Städtler, C., & Huron, D. (2020). *The psychological functions of music listening.* Frontiers in Psychology, 11, 1962.

Sharda, M., Sudha, M., & Sivakumar, P. T. (2021). *Effect of music therapy on social skills of children with autism spectrum disorder.* Journal of Indian Association for Child and Adolescent Mental Health, 17(1), 26-34.

Sharma, P. (2017). *Music therapy in ancient India.* Aarohi Publications.

Shukla, V. (2020). *Music therapy in psychiatric disorders.* Indian Journal of Psychological Medicine, 42(2), 102-107.

Silverman, M. J. (2020). *Music therapy in mental health: Contributions and challenges.* Psychiatric Times, 37(2), 15-17.

Silverman, M. J. (2020). *Music therapy in mental health: Contributions and challenges.* Psychiatric Times, 37 (2), 15-17.

Srinivasan, T. M., & Ramaratnam, S. (2019). *The current status of mental health services in India.* In Mental Health in South Asia (pp. 67-78). Springer, Singapore.

Vijayakumar, L., & John, S. (2019). *Suicide prevention in low-resource settings: A review of the current evidence of suicide prevention strategies and challenges in low-income countries.* In Suicide from Global Perspective: Psychological Approach (pp. 131-140). Springer, Cham.

24. Indian Knowledge System: A Way of Learning

Mr.Vikram Sharma & Dr. Bharat Gugane

Gurukula System

A gurukul or gurukulam is a type of education system in ancient India with shishya ('students' or 'disciples') living near or with the guru (teacher) in the same ashram (school) for a certain period of time where they learn and get educated by their guru. The word gurukula is a combination of the Sanskrit words guru ('teacher' or 'master') and kula ('family' or 'home').

The gurukul system of education has been in existence since ancient times. We find the instances of gurukulam in Upanishdas (philosophical-religious texts of Hinduism). The vedic school of thought prescribes the gurukula to all individuals before the age of 8 at least by 12. From initiation until the age of 25 all individuals are prescribed to be students and to remain unmarried, a celibate. This phase in one's life was also known as "Brahmacharyashram" which was one of the major four ashrams in ancient India. The students learn from the guru and help the guru in his everyday life, including carrying out of mundane daily household chores. The activities are not mundane and very essential part of the education to inculcate self-discipline among students. Typically, a guru does not receive or accept any fees from the shishya studying with him as the relationship between a guru and the shishya is considered very sacred.

At the end of one's education, a shishya offers the gurudakshina before leaving the gurukul. The gurudakshina is a traditional gesture of acknowledgement, respect and thanks to the guru, which may be monetary, but may also be a special task the teacher wants the student to accomplish. Through Gurukul, students used to learn self-discipline, politeness, good humanism and spirituality that would assist them to be an enlightened person in the future.

Modern Education System

The modern education system was introduced in 1835 by Lord Macauley, which was a British orient. In 1835, it was decided that western sciences and literature would be imparted to Indians through the medium of English by Lord William Bentinck's government. Bentinck had appointed Thomas Babington Macaulay as the Chairman of the General Committee of Public Instruction. Macaulay wished to create a class of Indians who were Indian in color and appearance but English in taste and affiliation. British Government imparted the Modern Education system in India because there was a huge demand for clerks and other administrative roles in the company's (East India Company) functioning.

Modern Education System in India brought so many reforms in Indian social – political – technical - economic – scientific sectors. In fact, scientific and technical education was ignored by the British government. Because their prime motive was to get cheaper laborers, specifically clerks for the smooth operations of their governance. No doubt it spread western education among Indians, but the rate of literacy was atrociously low during British rule. In 1911, the illiteracy rate in British India was 94%. In 1921, it was 92%. According to the data collected in 2018, India's literacy rate is 74%.

Key differences between Gurukula and Modern Education System in India

1 – Gurukula education system was devoted to the overall development of the student. Every professional was respected in the Gurukula system. Students learnt from the Gurukula were able to handle any kind of situation in their life as they were trained not only in academics but also in self-defense, spiritual and materialist improvement. On the other hand, in modern day's education we have seen maximum parents forcing their children to go for either medical studies or engineering as they are most prestigious or became lawyers. This is the mentality of the Indian Society.

2 – Activities such as Yoga, Meditation is never seen on the modern education system which was the inseparable part of the ancient Gurukul system for the moral and spiritual benefit of the pupil.

3 – We have a structured education system which is not meant for everyone. There is nothing the modern education system in India

provides that boost confidence, develop self-control, and discipline among the students else it demotivates them at every level creating psychological pressure which has indirectly affected the health of Indian students.

4 – In ancient times, we had prolific women scholars like Gargi, Maitreyi, Viswambhara and Apala. It proves that female education was promoted. But during the British rule, the state of women education was pathetic. This was because women could not generally be employed as clerks. In fact, women were not allowed to pursue higher education until 1920 and 1948 in Oxford and Cambridge Universities respectively.

Conclusion

The NEP 2020 has taken an initiative to modify the education system of India. They have promoted the use of regional languages and introduced vocational training. From now, marks will not play a significant role in the student's life but other factors will also count at the end of the year which will tell us about the performance of the student. The Gurukul system was the unique system of education which gave equal importance to all the sectors and developed persons who had radical and critical thinking ability with peace and confidence attitude which lacks in today's society. Mental and physical stability is very necessary for the gain of knowledge and implementing it in the professional life.

References

https://www.education.gov.in/nep/about-nep
mmc.ugc.ac.in
Retrieved from Wikipedia - https://en.wikipedia.org/wiki/Gurukula
https://worldpopulationreview.com/country-rankings/literacy-rate-by-country
"Gurukul System versus Modern Education in India – A Need for Amalgamation of the Two System to Eliminate the Crisis of Illiteracy, Economy and Social Problems of the Society" – International Journal of Recent Advances in Multidisciplinary Topics, Volume 2, Issue 11, November 2021.

25. New Education Policy, Culture and Languages

Dr. Sangeeta G. Avachar

Introduction

Language, undoubtedly, is a weapon for manifestation of human development. Since times immemorial language stands as one of the major weapons for advancement of human life. There are two types of communications as verbal and non-verbal communication. Until the invention of language scripts, non-verbal communication has been one of the significant means of conversation. However, with civilization gradual progress of human language scripts got developed showcasing language as a measure of articulation of human feelings leading to the enrichment of creative power. Ultimately, today, the innumerable languages developed over time being stand at the centre of advancement of human civilization enabling the manifestation of human potentials.

Nature of Problem

Why dissemination of knowledge through mother tongue/regional language is necessary and how far this will be attained through NEP-2020 so as to achieve cultural integrity through multilingualism is the concern of this study.

Obviously, language is an armament of human development, hence, almost all the societies of the world have incepted language artillery for marching ahead. In accordance with this tradition, India as a country also has accepted the significance of language advancements at various levels. India being a diverse geographical ensemblance is prone to multiple regional languages. Besides, a theory of imparting education through mother tongue springs as an effective theory for overall evolution of human potential. Thereby every regional language becomes equally significant bead in the multilingual thread of India. The three language formula is still in controversy with respect to the imposement of number of languages to be studied by the North, South, East, West and middle geographical locations of India. The teaching and learning of English as a foreign language has already added innovative dimensions to the scene of cultural integrity of the country. On the global scene, English nodoubt has acquired the status of language of world knowledge, however, the necessity of catering education through regional language/ mother tongue also has been scientifically proved. Moreover, for creating a balance between these two situations India aspires to find a cosmopolitan approach by focusing the essentiality to offer education through mother tongue at least at the primary level. Educationists and thinkers like Rabindranath Tagore had stressed the need for imparting primary education in mother tongue. And stepping ahead, it has been determined to righteously accept multilingualism by juxtaposing regional languages in the journey of catering education. It has been admitted by Prof Neelima Gupta, the Vice Chancellor of Harisingh Gaur University, Sagar, Madhya Pradesh that NEP-2020 is based on multidisciplinary approach, the facilities of multiple entry and exit, and credit framework in one of her conversations with National Skills Framework, these characteristics of NEP-2020 spectacularly go hand in hand with India's multilingual diversity.

National Education Policies of a country do frame, implement, monitor and review the education system. Before NEP-2020 India implemented two education policies. The first education policy of India implemented in the year 1968 spoke about the regional languages in addition to Three Language formula. India's second education policy of 1986 worked in the same line of the first policy. It spoke about decoding a policy outline for education in mother tongue at the Secondary stage. The third and latest education policy NEP-2020 in accordance with the National values framework of India has planned for the holistic education to achieve cultural and national integrity. Adverently, NEP-2020 emphasized on catering primary education through mother tongue prominently by allocating due weightage to multilingualism and resultant translation studies.

Universally, education is accepted as a fundamental tool for shaping full human potential, developing an equitable and just society for the attainment of country's aspiring progress. This can be achieved by universal access to quality education that can be fruitfully incepted through the language of the people. On the other side, in India, any one language is unable to acquire the position of a national language, hence, there is a division as such that till date 22 languages are official languages for different states and Hindi and English have flourished as the two official languages of the nation.

Inferentially, India as a nation displays multilingualism as a major characteristic owing to its diversity. Hence, National Education Policies of India automatically emphasized their effective implementation by appropriately focusing education through regional languages. Accordingly, the effective implementation of NEP-2020 has to be carried out in order to meticulously shape the future of this nation as it is said, "Future of a country is shaped in its classrooms." National Education Policy 2020 offers flexibility in course choices, accordingly, it adheres multilingualism and the power of learning languages for effective dissemination of education at every level from primary to higher. Educationists, philosophers, studies and research have focused that primary education should be disseminated through mother tongue and/or regional language because the full human potential gets blossomed through the medium of mother tongue for a child. It is accepted and approved that children learn and grasp any concept quickly in their mother tongue or home language that are normally the languages of local communities. However, there might be alterations in this regard.

According to National Education Policy 2020:

"Whereever possible, the medium of instruction until at least Grade 5, but preferably till Grade 8 and beyond will be the home language/mother tongue/local Language/regional language. Thereafter, the home/local language shall continue to be taught as a language wherever possible." (NEP 2020, p.13).

This recommendation of NEP-2020 is in harmony with India's multilingualism, diverse cultures and varied civilizations. Besides, multilingualism is the need of today's global scenario. It is obvious that multilingual speakers outnumber monolingual speakers in the world's census. It is crystal clear that many countries on the globe have chosen multilingual contexts for imparting education. Streamlining with this cosomopolitan demand, the recommendation of NEP-2020 for the deliberate choice of home language is a welcome gesture. Its implementation has been made mandatory for both public and private schools. for assisting this very purpose text books including those of science will be made available in home language/mother tongue. The provision has been done for special attention to bridge the gaps between the languages spoken by the child and medium of teaching if such gap exists. If the home language text books or material is not available, even then, the language of conversation between teachers and students will be the home language whereever possible to the utmost level. Teachers are expected to inculcate bilingual teaching-learning methods and materials for the students with different mother tongues and medium of instruction. All languages will be taught with high quality to all students, whether they fall in the category of medium of instruction or else. This move is effectively going to promote bilingualism and multilingualism leading to cultural integrity that ultimately takes the civilizations towards national integrity.

National Integration can be defined as generating a mental outlook that guides, encourages and facilitates a person to prioritize the loyalty to a country above group loyalties and reflects the welfare of the country above narrow secterian interests. In short weaving different civilizations and people into one thread harmoniously is the essence of National Integration that is attainable through the recommendation of NEP-2020 regarding language policy.

NEP-2020 focuses on multilingualism as a cognitive benefit to young students adhering to research inferences that the children pick up languages extremely quickly between age 2 to 8, accordingly it has structured an exposition of different languages for the early age group with priority thrust on mother tongue initiating it from foundation level. It will be systematically executed to continue the teaching-learning of languages in a delightful manner by establishing proper communion with targeted attention on skill development upto Grade 3 and beyond. This scenario regarding language teaching-learning is going to facilitate with wonderful opportunities to teacher community as governments from Centre to State decide to invest in language teachers almost in all regional languages mentioned in the Eighth Schedule of the Constituion of India. Additionally, bilateral agreements for hiring language teachers may enter into effect to assist the three language formula in different states and ultimately to accelerate prospectus of Indian languages across the country. Technosavvy teaching-learning of different languages will also enhance interests in language learning strengthening cultural and ultimately national integrity.

NEP-2020 centres around the three language formula with respect to the Constitutional provisions, aspirations of the people, regions and the need to promote multilingualism, heading towards national integrity. However, our experiences regarding three language formula and fruitlessness of any imposement and insistence with respect to languag studies, students are given full liberty to change one or more of the three languages during Grade 6 or 7 as long as they are able to display basic proficiency in three languages by the end of secondary school. For facilitating the students in a fruitful manner NEP-2020 has proposed and recommended high quality bilingual text books and teaching-learning equipments as well as entire substance so that students will be enabled to think and voice their say about these two essential subjects both in their home language and in English.

Juxtaposing the importance of regional languages and multilingualism through NEP-2020 for educational, social and technological advancements will be of immense benefit for the aspirants of knowledge. Acquing education in one's own language and culture had never been a detriment to human development in the broader perspectives, moreover, India's languages are among the richest, most scientific, most appealing and most expressive languages in the world. Rich heritage of the Indian languages facilitates access to enormous culture of India through the artillery of literature, music and so on and so forth familiarizing with national identity and character. Hence, taking into consideration the demand of awareness about the affluent and extensive constellation about the tongues and the treasures of India as a nation leading it towards cultural enrichment and national integration NEP-2020 has meticulously decided over its language policies, however, effective implementation of the policy only is going to offer outcome based results.

In order to make language learning interesting the provision for a fun project/activity on 'The Languages of India' is scheduled through NEP-2020 sometime in Grades 6-8 under 'Ek Bharat Shreshta Bharat' initiative. This will enable learning of major Indian Languages with a focus on their remarkable unity adhering to their commonalities in many respects. Geographical language veracity and the study of tribal languages will support this endeavour. Sanskrit and other classical languages have been imparted vibrant weightage during Grades 6-12 where students can have an option of learning at least two years of a classical language and its literature by way of exposure to experiential innovative approaches integrating with technology. This will be a continuation from the middle stage through the secondary and beyond.

NEP-2020 not only proposes the study of languages of Indian origin but also offers foreign languages from secondary level onwards. Ours is a philosophy of 'Vasudhaiv Kutumbkam', streamlining with this philosophy our students will be enriched with global knowledge about world cultures with mobility according to their own interests and aspirations. Different art forms will be utilized to enhance teaching of languages. Additionally, Indian Sign Language will be standardized accross the country as per NEP-2020 recommendations and accordingly, National and State curriculum materials are going to be structured for use of students with hearing impairment. Local sign languages also are going to be taught as and when possible and relevant.

Conclusion

NEP-2020, based on freedom, flexibility and choices, through its implementation envisages the wide ranging opportunites being incepted in the educational scenario of the world's biggest education system. At present it caters to the educational demands of near about 300 million students, in future it is going to deal with approximately 500 million students. Based on multiple entry and exit, adhering to credit framework and modelled on skill enhancements, NEP 2020 is flexible, spot lighting teacher quality and human resources, indeed, it is the most desired policy due to its remarkable focus on skill orientation and industry linkage based education. Highlighting regional language as a medium of instruction and multilinguality are definately facilitating new horizons in language education. The provision for being multilingual leads to cultural understanding and national integration. Conversion of text books and study materials into regional languages have posed tremendous opportunities in the field of translation creating new vistas for teachers and translators. No doubt there are some drawbacks and lacunas in overall and a few obstacles are being faced in the process of implementation, however, while following language recommendations, tolerance towards multilinguality and inclination towards being multilingual are going to assist entire stakeholders. Any change is little bit hectic at the initial stage and in the process of implementation many obstacles will be met with remedies. With due weightage to foreign languages, NEP-2020 intends to head towards internationalization of education by facilitating digitalization as its primary demand. NEP-2020 hopes to convert educational aspirants into critical thinkers, problem solvers and solution providers according to UGC acting Chairman M. Jagdesh Kumar, and languages are decisively going to be proved immensely beneficial in this marching ahead. The states like Karnataka, Madhya Pradesh, Uttar Pradesh, Telangana, Andhra Pradesh, Rajasthan, Assam and Maharashtra have implemented NEP-2020 till date in spite of some obstacles to it and are trying to overcome those hurdles based on the suggestions of educationists, philosophers, thinkers and stakeholders. They are meticulously trying to overcome lacunas by imparting motivation to the masses for its effective implementation with prominent role of each of their regional language.

References

Das, Prasenjit & Das, Gouri & Barman, Pranab. (2023). *National Education Policy 2020: Current Issues and Reimagining the Future of Higher Education*. International Journal of Indian Psychology. 11. 3880-3889. 10.25215/1103.360.

https://indiaeducationdiary.in/highlights-of-new-education-policy-2020/

https://www.academia.edu/33372299/National_Integration_in_Multiling ual_and_Multicultural_Context_A_Case_of_India

https://www.youtube.com/watch?v=GPy4wHKikLs (Conversation)

https://youtu.be/Z21EBx4ktKs?si=f9jWvpvg73ijPO3M (Conversation)

India Education Diary. Highlights of New Education Policy 2020.

Koul, Omkar N. 2005. *National Integration in Multilingual and Multicultural Context: A Case Study of India*. Indian Institute of Language Studies. Cited via academia.edu

More, D. N. 2023. *Uccha Shikshan Dhoran: Avhane Ani Disha*. (Marathi Language) Pune: The Unique Foundation Social Intervention Through Education.

NEP (2020): Policy document released by Government of India
Retrieved from
https://www.education.gov.in/sites/upload_files/mhrd/files/NEP_Fina
l_English_0.pdf

26. Myth, Modernity and Karmic Retribution in Popular Culture: A Study of Mike Flanagan's The Fall of the House of Usher

Shweta Sarkar & Puja Sarmah

Introduction

Pop culture, or popular culture, is a term that refers to the entirety of ideas, perspectives, attitudes, memes, images, and other phenomena that are within the mainstream of a given culture. It encompasses the most prevalent aspects of contemporary society, including music, fashion, movies, television, literature, sports, and other aspects of daily life that are widely embraced and celebrated by a large majority of people in a particular society. Overall, Popular culture has a major impact on society's beliefs, values, and sense of self. It mirrors the shared beliefs and values of a particular society or community at a given time and is continually changing due to factors such as technological advancements, globalization, and demographic shifts.

In this context, The National Education Policy (NEP) 2020 in India acknowledges the significance of popular culture in shaping the educational landscape. While the policy recognizes the significance of popular culture in shaping the educational landscape and enriching the learning experience of students. It emphasizes the critical role of popular culture in fostering creativity, critical thinking, and social awareness among students. It acknowledges the potential of popular culture to provide a platform for exploring diverse perspectives, promoting inclusivity, and building cultural competence. The policy also recognizes that popular culture can help bridge the gap between formal education and informal learning. It encourages the integration of popular media, arts, and literature into the curriculum to create a more engaging and relevant learning experience for students. Furthermore, the NEP 2020 emphasizes the need to promote cultural exchange and diversity in education recognizing that popular culture can facilitate cross-cultural understanding and appreciation, helping to promote a more harmonious and inclusive society.

The horror series The Fall of the House of Usher, created by Mike Flanagan, captures the attention of viewers worldwide with its engaging narrative and thought-provoking mythological interpretation. This series skillfully intertwines the contemporary issue of the opioid crisis with the story of the Usher family, who are involved in the pharmaceutical industry. It is important to note that this adaptation loosely draws from Edgar Allen Poe's renowned short story and explores modern versions of his classic poetry.

Individuals consistently turn to historical retrospection as a means of rational examination. Authors frequently observe an intriguing connection between their literary works and the ancient myths of their society. Amidst a collection of anecdotes, the incorporation of these mythological elements provides them with a sense of liberation and fulfillment in their artistic expression. What is a myth? M.H. Abrams define myth as "In its central modern significance, however, a myth is one story in a mythology—a system of hereditary stories of ancient origin which were once believed to be true by a particular cultural group, and which served to explain (in terms of the intentions and actions of deities and other supernatural beings) why the world is as it is and things happen as they do, to provide a rationale for social customs and observances, and to establish the sanctions for the rules by which people conduct their lives". (2012, 230).

One of the most notable references in this series is to Poe's poem, 'The Raven'. The raven has long held a significant place in various mythologies and is commonly associated with themes of death and fortune. The myth surrounding the raven is intricate, yet it consistently symbolizes prophecy and insight. The true nature of Raven in "The Fall of the House of Usher" remains enigmatic yet thought-provoking. The character Verna, portrayed by Carla Gugino, symbolizes the Raven through her anagram and plays a significant role in each episode, bringing about the culmination of each member of the Usher family. The narrative revolves around the Usher family, specifically the twins Roderick and Madeline Usher, portrayed by Bruce Greenwood and Mary McDonnell respectively, along with their numerous offspring. As the family members tragically meet their demise, a notable observation emerges – a mysterious woman, perpetually unaged, appears to be intricately associated with each death.

Paired with Raven imagery, Verna takes on the form of a shape-shifting demonic figure that foretells events and provides subtle warnings to the characters before their demise, embodying the characteristics typically associated with the Raven such as insights, prophecy, death, and fortune. In the second episode of the series titled "The Masque of the Red Death," Verna initiates her first interaction with Prospero, portrayed by Saurian Sapkota, who is one of the illegitimate sons of the Ushers and unfortunately the first one to meet his demise. Verna mysteriously appears at the rave party and entices Prospero to accompany her to the bedroom. Once there, she delivers a vague and enigmatic warning, stating, "Consequence, and tonight is consequential." (Flangan, 2023, 50:30). Subsequently, she vanishes as abruptly as a speck of dust. Soon after, the sprinkler system unexpectedly activates, which the youngest Usher child anticipates will enhance the liveliness of the night. However, the substance that cascades from above is not water, but actually acid obtained from a Fortunato Pharmaceutical laboratory. This causes the skin of all the attendees to painfully burn off and their ultimate demise. This incident clearly exemplifies her warning statement and the conventional symbolic traits of the raven.

Derived from the Sanskrit word karm, 'karma' refers to the concept of action, work, or deed and its consequences. However, in Indian religions, karma is more than just a simple cause-andeffect relationship. It is a principle that governs the way individuals live their lives. Karmic retribution suggests that the person who performs an action is held responsible and accountable for it. Acts that have moral or ritual importance will bring about their own reward or punishment, which can be favourable or unfavourable experiences. Hence, recurring on multiple occasions, Verna repeatedly emerges to aggravate the deaths of the Usher's offspring, assuming different forms and appearances. This establishes Verna as something beyond a mere human, but rather a supernatural entity possessing considerable power to enforce karmic retribution upon the characters. Taking the form of a raven, she systematically preys on each member of the Usher family, resulting in their demise. The presence of the Raven in the downfall of the House of

Usher establishes a literary connection to Poe's fictional realm and his imaginative writing.

Symbolizing *karma,* Verna serves as a reminder of the interconnectedness between actions and their consequences, emphasising the principle of reaping what one sows. As the show nears its conclusion, it is revealed that Verna's continual and ever-present involvement with the Usher family is tied to the fateful night in 1980 when the twins, Roderick and Madeline, formed a pact with her. Roderick and Madeleine are in need of an alibi as they have recently committed the act of murder against their employer at Fortunato Pharmaceuticals. Verna is aware of this wrongdoing and confronts them, proposing a bargain, "You get the whole world, and when you're done, at the end of it all…your bloodline dies with you" (Flanagan, 2023, 30:28). In exchange for unlimited fame and wealth, Roderick and Madeleine must agree to the extinction of their bloodline upon their deaths, ensuring that any offspring or descendants meet the same fate. The Ushers quickly agree to accept Verna's offer without much deliberation. The twins depart from the bar during the early morning hours; however, upon looking back, they discover the absence of the establishment. In its place stands a brick wall adorned with graffiti, depicting a raven at its apex. Once again, the raven's mythological significance is emphasised, symbolising its ability to bestow fortune or bring about death. This occurrence further accentuates the potency of illusions, causing them to question whether their perception of reality is distorted or if their conscience is reminding them of the consequences that karma may manifest as a result of their actions.

The Fall of the House of Usher is a prime example of Gothic literature in which the story delves deep into the Gothic tradition that has been prevalent in Western literature for centuries. However, Poe's innovation and development have added a modern touch to the story, making it unique and timeless. The story's psychological analysis is one of its most striking elements, a hallmark of Poe's writing. Each episode of the series offers a profound understanding of the psychological challenges faced by individuals in our modern society. The advancement of social software and industrial civilization has led to a shift in human communication towards virtual environments. This shift has resulted in people becoming more independent, self-centred, and introspective. Consequently, it has led to various psychological issues such as loneliness, alienation, and personality fragmentation. The current situation has made people reflect on the impact of technology on modern society.

The Usher family, despite their wealth and status, seem to have a peculiar obsession with their own establishment. Be it art, technology, or business, each member of the family pours all their energy and resources into their respective pursuits, often without considering the repercussions of their actions on the common people. As a result, their creations, which are meant to enrich their lives, often end up causing harm to others. For instance, Victorine, another illegitimate child of Roderick Usher played by T'nia Miller in the episode "The Tell-Tale Heart" is facing the daunting challenge of proving her worth by making her father's investment in her latest invention, the mesh heart, a resounding success. Despite the pressure, Victorine is determined to succeed and prove her mettle in the competitive world of inventions. Seeking support for her father's investment, she confidently turned to her girlfriend and partner Alessandra Ruiz (Paola Núñez), for help. Unfortunately, the situation escalated into a heated argument over questionable medical trials and fraudulent documents for a human trial. Victorine hurled a bookend at Alessandra with full force, hitting her squarely in the back of the head as she attempted to leave. Realising that she just killed the woman she loved, Victorine sliced her body open and installed the prototype to Alessandra's heart, leaving it beating uselessly. This episode ends with Victorine stabbing her own heart in front of her father. Eventually, karma was at work again, as Victorine experimented with her heart prototype on numerous defenceless animals, killing them in the process.

Flanagan's adaptation of Poe's two short stories "The Gold Bug" and "Tamerlane" put together in the episode "The Gold Bug" features the character of Roderick's first-born daughter Tamerlane aka Tammy (Samantha Sloyan). Tammy is so self-obsessed with herself and her reputation of being an Usher that she even turns down her fitness model and husband, Billy during the launch of their health and wellness product. Left alone with her work, she is so stressed that she hallucinates, fumbles and ruins her dream project at the launch event. Being repeatedly taunted by Verna in the mirror, Tammy smashes all the mirrors in the house with a fire poker and ends up impaled by both. The irony is that Tammy, the self-obsessed person started hating the sight of herself and was ultimately killed by her own reflection.

Conclusion

It can be concluded by saying that popular culture serves as a valuable resource for enhancing the quality and relevance of education as envisioned in the National Education Policy 2020. By embracing the diverse forms of popular culture, educators can create inclusive, engaging, and meaningful learning experiences that empower students to thrive in a rapidly changing world. The policy's emphasis on integrating popular culture into education can help create a more engaging, relevant, and inclusive learning environment that nurtures students' creativity and critical thinking.

References

National Education Policy 2020, Ministry of Human Resource Development, Govt. of India.

https://www.education. gov. in/sites/upload_files /mhrd/files/ NEP_Final_ English_0.pdf.

Barry, P. (2018). Beginning theory: An introduction to literary and cultural theory. New Delhi, Viva Books.

Flanagan, M. (Director). (2023). The Fall of the House of Usher (miniseries). The Newton Brothers. Netflix. https://www.netflix.com/

Abrams, M.H. & Harpham, G. G (2012). *A Glossary of Literary Terms*. Delhi, Cenage Learning.

Powell, J.L. (2015). *Foucault, power and culture*. International journal of humanities and cultural studies, 401-419. http://ijhcschiefeditor.wix.com/ijhcs

27. NEP 2020: Transforming Commerce Education

Dr. K. M. Gholap

Introduction

The policy envisages broad-based, multi- disciplinary, holistic Under Graduate education with flexible curricula, creative combinations of subjects, integration of vocational education and multiple entry and exit points with appropriate certification. The current higher education system is plagued by various issues, including fragmentation, a deficiency of cognitive skills development, rigid disciplinary divisions, restricted access, unfocused research and inadequate governance. NEP-2020 provides a comprehensive framework for primary education to include teaching business & technical education. It also got provision for internet-based e-leanings which is paradigm shift from conventional system. The essence of NEP is access, equity, affordability, responsibility, and quality in accordance with United Nations sustainable goals. NEP is not free from loopholes, but it has taken deep insight into global scenario. It should be implemented with great caution to address challenges that are required for fostering quality education for all.

Review

Education plays a strong role in building nation; education decides the future of the nation, the destiny of its people. The impact is going to be a durable one in terms of growth and development of the state and subject. The role of education and its importance can't be ignored in today's scenario. Taina Saarinen (2008) has addressed the text and discourse analysis in education policy from theoretical and methodological points of view. Policies are discursive processes, and it disputes instruction policies. Policy documents can be used as information, and it is seen usually in the case in instruction policy analysis. Deb, P. (2020) discussed the Indian ethos and cultural values in teaching that got its place in National Education Policy (NEP) 2020. Suryavanshi, S. (2020)

has stressed upon development of teacher in Indian universities on Chinese university model. It emphasized that autonomy should be provided to college and university teachers to decide their teaching methodology and support should be provided for research, and innovation.

Guidelines of NEP-2020

Under the new structure students will be awarded the UG Certificate after the first year 40-44 credits, the UG diploma after the second year 80-88 credits and bachelor's degree after the third year 120-132 credits and with the honours 160-176 credits. The distribution of curriculum across four-year degree programme will be divided into six verticals i.e.

Major (Core) Subject	Minor Subject	Open Elective Course (OEC)	Vocational and Skill Enhancement Courses (VSEC)	Ability Enhancement Courses (AEC) Indian Knowledge System (IKS) and Value Education Courses (VEC)	Field Projects/ Internship/ Apprenticeship/ Community Engagement & Service corresponding to the Major (Core) Subject, Co-curricular Courses (CC) And Research Project
Minimum 50% of total credits corresponding to Three/Four - years UG Degree	18-20 Credits Faculty (core)	10-12 credits	14-16 credits	14 credits	20-24 credits

(source: Sukanu Committee Report 2022)

The National Education Policy-2020 laid a roadmap for progressive education keeping essence of ancient ethos of Indian tradition, culture, values, to build new country with futuristic vision. India has got rich historical heritage with education rooted in it since ages. NEP 2020 is formulated after wide consultations with stakeholders from all the sectors. It is aimed to provide multi-disciplinary skill-based education to generate employment; It is aimed at increasing enrolment of students in all kinds of educational institutions by 2030. This will require massive changes in present conventional education system. Hence, it also needs to introduce accountability of each stakeholder at all levels.

Conclusion

The paper concludes by highlighting the progressive nature of NEP 2020, its alignment with the changing socio-economic landscape, and its role in equipping students with skills-set needed for the digital age. It emphasizes the need for effective implementation and integration with other government initiatives. The paper draws from various sources, including government documents, reports, and expert opinions, to provide a detailed analysis. It discusses the potential benefits of NEP 2020 in terms of improving education quality, offering flexibility to students, promoting innovation, and aligning education with global standards. Overall, it seems to offer a comprehensive understanding of NEP 2020's implications for higher education in India, presenting both the opportunities and challenges associated with its implantation.

References

Dr. Sheetal B. Kale, "*NEP 2020 & Commerce & Management Education*" International Journal of Commerce and Management Studies (IJCAMS) Peer Reviewed, Indexed Journal, ISSN 2456-3684 Vol.8, No.1, 2023, www.ijcams.com Pp-477

Praveen Jha, Pooja Parvati, (2020), "*Long on Rhetoric and Short on substance National Education Policy, 2020*", Economic and Political review journal, Vol. 55, Issue No. 34.

Dr. Laxmikant Puri, "*National Edn Policy 2020 to transform UG Education*" Lokmat Times -News, Dt. 14th Feb 2024.

Alok Kumar, "*New education policy (NEP) 2020: A roadmap for India 2.0*" University of South Florida (USF) M3 Publishing.

Contributors

Dr. Rajesh S. Gore
Head, Department of English, Toshniwal Arts, Commerce & Science College, Sengaon, Dist. Hingoli (MS)
rsgore5880@gamil.com, Contact No. 7972821329

Dr. Pranjali Bhanudas Vidyasagar
Head, Department of English,
Sanskar Mandir Sanstha's Arts & Commerce College, Pune
pranjalividyasagar@gmail.com, Contact No. 9359072335/ 9921433456

Rajendrakumar Ahirrao
Department of Physics, Uttamrao Patil Arts and Science College, Dahiwel, Tal. Sakri, Dist-Dhule, Pin:424302, Maharashtra, India

Narender Paul
Department of Physics, Govt. Degree College, Ani (at. Haripur) Dist-Kullu, Himachal Pradesh, India

Arjun Namdevrao Khobragade
Assistant Professor, Department of English, Yeshwant Mahavidyalaya, Seoo, Dist. Wardha, Email: arjunkhobragade@gmail.com
Mobile No. 9850307101

Dr. Harsha Suryawanshi
Assistant Professor, Shri Shivaji Law College, Parbhani

Dr. Shilpa Deshpande
Chishtiya College of Arts, Science and Commerce, Khuldabad, Aurangabad (shilpap.khot@gmail.com)

Dr. Munjaji K. Rakhonde
Associate Professor and Head, Department of Psychology, Kohinoor Arts Commerce & Science College. Khultabad. Dist. Chhatrapati Sambhajinagar, Email: Rakhundemk155@gmail.com

S.N. Lokhande, P.U. Bhalchandra, S.R. Mekewad and S.D. Khamitkar

School of Computational Sciences, S.R.T.M. University, Nanded, MS, 431606, India, lokhandesn19@gmail.com, srtmun.parag@gmail.com, satishmekewad@gmail.com, s.khamitkar@gmail.com

Sachin M. Narangale
Assistant Professor, School of Media Studies, Swami Ramanand Teerth Marathwada University, Nanded, sachin.narangale@srtmun.ac.in

Dr. Deepak Subhabh Waghmare
Head & Research Supervisor, Department of Public Administration, Pratibha Niketan College, Nanded (MS), Mo. 9822033819

Dr. Suchita Suragihalli
Assistant Professor, Shahaji Law College, Kolhapur, Mob: 8600493498

Dr. Pandit B. Nirmal
Assistant Professor and Head, Department of English, Sant Tukaram College of Arts and Science, Basmat Road, Parbhani 431401 Maharashtra India, panditbnirmal@gmail.com

Anirudhha Pimpalgaonka, Parag Bhalchandra & Gajanan Kurundkar
Data Operator, Department of Examinations, S.R.T.M. University, Nanded, MS, 431606, India, asppimp@gmail.com
School of Computational Sciences, S.R.T.M. University, Nanded, MS, 431606, India, srtmun.parag@gmail.com
Dept. of Computer Science, SGBS College, Purna(Jn), Dist Parbhani, MS, India, gajanankurundkar@gmail.com

Jyothi Gedela
PhD Scholar from Amity University, Maharashtra

Dr. Swati Bhise
Assistant Professor, Amity University, Maharashtra

Mr. Kailas Baburao Tidke
Research Scholar, Dr. B. A. M. University, Aurangabad, tidkekailas1@gmail.com Cell. No. 9881994736

Dr. Ramesh Bhanudas Jaybhaye
Research Supervisor, Dadojirao Deshmukh Arts, com. and Sci. College, Waluj, Aurangabad rameshbjaybhaye@gmail.com

Dhrumi Shah
Research Scholar, Amity University, Panvel, Maharashtra

Dr. Ramkishan Bhise
Assistant Professor, SIES Graduate School of Technology, Nerul, Navi Mumbai, Email ID: ram.bhise2009@gmail.com

Dr. Parag Bhalchandra, Dr. Vaijayanta Patil, Dr. Mahesh Joshi, & Dr. Ashok Gingine
School of Computational Sciences, S.R.T.M. Universit, Nanded, MS, 431606, India
School of Educational Sciecnes, S.R.T.M. University, Nanded, MS, 431606, India srtmun.parag@gmail.com vaijayantapatil@gmail.com maheshmj25@gmail.com apgingine@gmail.com

Dr. Manisha Kale
Associate Professor, Department of English, Pratishthan Mahavidyalaya Paithan, manishabkale@gmail.com

Dr. Dipak Wayal
Assistant Professor, Ness Wadia College of Commerce, Pune dipakwayal@gmail.com

Dr. Nirmala S. Padmavat
Assistant Professor of English and Director IQAC, Nutan Mahavidyalaya, Selu drnspadmavat@gmail.com

Dr. Ramakant Dnyanobarao Mundhe
Assistant Professor of English, Sant Tukaram College of Arts and Science, Parbhani, raman007mundhe@gmail.com Mo. 9423444453

Ms. Durva Kishor Mandrekar
Assistant Professor in English, Ganpat Parsekar College of Education, Harmal-Goa, Mo. 9689382809 durvamandrekar@gmail.com

Satish Mekewad, Santosh Khamitkar, Sakharam Lokhande & Parag Bhalchandra
School of Computational Sciences, S.R.T.M. University, Nanded, MS, 431606, India satishmekewad@gmail.com, srtmun.parag@gmail.com, s_khamitkar@yahoo.com, snlokhande19@gmail.com

Mr. Vikram Sharma & Dr. Bharat Gugane
Bhonsala Military College, Nashik

Dr. Sangeeta G. Avachar
HoD, English, L. S. K. J. Mahila Mahavidyalaya, Parbhani, Maharashtra (India) Mo. 9767323290, sgavachar.1976@gmail.com

Puja Sarmah
Research Scholar, Department of English, Assam University Diphu Campus, Assam, 8638461317, pujasarmah9@gmail.com

Shweta Sarkar
Assistant Professor, Department of English, Bokajan College, Assam, 9365892825, sarkarshweta8@gmail.com

Dr. K. M. Gholap
JETs Z. B. Patil College, Dhule (MS)